Praise for
Internal Family Systems Couple Therapy Skills Manual

"This Internal Family Systems manual on couples therapy clearly describes and illustrates how an IFS couples therapist works with clear and useful exercises for couples at home and after therapy. Therapists working from this perspective, and well as from other modalities, will be informed and enriched by its depth and thoroughness and couples will be expertly guided around the interface of their interacting 'parts'."

— **Harville Hendrix, PhD** and **Helen LaKelly Hunt, PhD**,
authors of *Getting the Love You Want*

"Herbine-Blank and Sweezy's manual is elegantly simple and stunningly profound. Therapeutic models are often easier to teach than they are to integrate into one's own therapeutic practice. This manual shows us how to utilize their treatment model, Intimacy from the Inside Out, and the myriad of case examples shows us the amazing results. Couple after couple is able to let down their guard and learn how to open their hearts to each other with tenderness and compassion. Bateson famously said, "The map is not the territory." But this book is a map that is as close to being in the room with IFIO's masters as one could hope to be. It's a treasure map. It could transform your practice."

— **David Treadway, PhD**, therapist, educator, author of
Treating Couples Well, A Practical Guide to Collaborative Couple Therapy

"IFIO provides a necessary bridge between differentiation and attachment, empowering therapists to sharpen their therapeutic focus and effectiveness in facilitating healing conversations."

— **George Faller, LMFT, EFT Trainer,** founder and president of the
New York Center for Emotionally Focused Therapy

Internal Family Systems

Couple Therapy Skills Manual

Healing Relationships with Intimacy From the Inside Out

Toni Herbine-Blank, MSN, RN & Martha Sweezy, PhD

Copyright © 2021 by Toni Herbine-Blank & Martha Sweezy

Published by
PESI Publishing
3839 White Ave
Eau Claire, WI 54703

Cover: Amy Rubenzer
Editing: Jenessa Jackson, PhD
Layout: Amy Rubenzer & Bookmasters

ISBN: 9781683733676
All rights reserved.

Printed in the United States of America

PESI Publishing
pesipublishing.com

About the Authors

Toni Herbine-Blank, MSN, RN

Toni Herbine-Blank, MSN, RN, is a senior trainer for the IFS-Institute and the sole developer for the Intimacy from the Inside Out training programs. She runs couple therapy training programs, retreats, and workshops nationally and internationally, and has co-authored the book *Intimacy from the Inside Out: Courage and Compassion in Couple Therapy*. She lives with her family in Durango Colorado. www.toniherbineblank.com

Martha Sweezy, PhD

Martha Sweezy, PhD, is an assistant professor at Harvard Medical School, a program consultant and supervisor at Cambridge Health Alliance, and the former assistant director and director of training for the dialectical behavioral therapy (DBT) program at the Cambridge Health Alliance. She is co-author of *Internal Family Systems Therapy; The IFS Skills Training Manual: Trauma-Informed Treatment for Anxiety, Depression, PTSD & Substance Abuse; Intimacy from the Inside Out: Courage and Compassion in Couple Therapy*. She is also an author and the co-editor for *Innovations and Elaborations in Internal Family Systems Therapy* and *Internal Family Systems Therapy: New Dimensions*. She has written articles on IFS for the *Journal of Psychotherapy Integration* and the *American Journal of Psychotherapy*. She has a therapy and consultation practice in Northampton, Massachusetts.

Dedication

I dedicate this book to my husband, Jordan, for his continual love and support; my horse, Redhawk, for asking me to stay congruent; and my dog, Waylon, who gives me a pass every time.

— **Toni Herbine-Blank**

I dedicate my work in this book to my siblings and their partners who are my dear friends and life companions: Sam Sweezy and Susan Callaghan, and Lybess Sweezy and Ken Miller.

— **Martha Sweezy**

Table of Contents

Acknowledgments

When I met Toni Herbine-Blank at an IFS training 21 years ago, I was impressed with her aptitude for the IFS model and asked her to consider becoming a trainer. Happily, she agreed. Already an experienced couple therapist, Toni was drawn to my IFS couple therapy framework and soon approached me about developing IFS-based couple therapy training. The result, Intimacy from the Inside Out (IFIO), is now a high quality, well-established national and international program. While developing this exceptional training opportunity, Toni remained steadfastly committed to the mission of IFS. Known for her clarity and courage, she is beloved in the IFS community as a teacher, colleague, and friend. Her contributions have been tremendous. I'm very grateful.

— **Richard C. Schwartz, PhD, founder of IFS**

I thank Martha Sweezy for her exquisite writing, editing, and collaboration. To my dedicated IFIO staff, Cathy Curtis, Ann Drouilhet, Kate Lingren, Joanne Gaffney, John Palmer, Larry Rosenberg, Robin Warsh, Nancy Wonder, and Judi Zoldan, I extend my deepest appreciation. Sincere thanks goes to Dick Schwartz for the IFS model and Jon Schwartz for his ongoing championing of IFIO. Many thanks to Linda Jackson and Jenessa Jackson of PESI for their support, expertise, and patience. And finally, thank you to my family and friends for their constant validation and encouragement.

— Toni Herbine-Blank

Toni is a delightful, wise, and generous collaborator. I thank her for that and for giving me the opportunity to co-author a manual on IFIO. As always, I thank my partner, Rob Postel, for his kindness and love. And I'm grateful to Linda Jackson and Jenessa Jackson of PESI for their support.

— Martha Sweezy

Introduction

Toni Herbine-Blank developed the couple therapy Intimacy from the Inside Out (IFIO) as a branch of Internal Family Systems (IFS) therapy, a treatment used for individuals, couples, families, communities, and organizations. Intimate relationships inevitably pose painful dilemmas and require partners to navigate differences. If they cannot differentiate and stay connected in the process, they end up experiencing, as Dan Seigel wrote, emotional chaos or rigidity (2007). IFIO is designed to help partners differentiate and stay connected by accessing their strengths (Herbine-Blank, Kerpelman, & Sweezy, 2016). When we speak and listen skillfully, we deepen and transform our relationships. In IFIO, we aim for partners to disagree respectfully, communicate courageously, apologize from the heart, forgive freely, and stay connected. Loving connection leads to ongoing well-being.

This book walks readers through the flow of IFIO descriptively and experientially, weaving interpersonal communication techniques with deep intrapsychic exploration. It guides therapists and couples to intervene effectively in patterns of conflict, move from protective power struggles to vulnerable conversations without attack or silence, and use an essential IFS technique called *unblending* to understand themselves and others.

In the first section, we introduce the conceptual underpinnings of IFIO, including the idea that we all have motivated, active subpersonalities (or *parts*), who influence our views and behavior, and two easily accessible, crucial skills: (1) differentiating (or *unblending*) from parts in order to be in relationship with them and (2) attending internally (or doing a *U-turn*) in order to help parts in moments of reactivity.

In the second section, we provide step-by-step techniques, case examples, and exercises for use with clients in each phase of IFIO treatment. Phase one: We connect with the couple, assesses their relational dynamics, introduce them to IFIO, and start befriending their protective parts. Phase two: We track patterns of conflict and help partners unblend so they can speak for parts and listen from the heart. We aim for the couple to appreciate the inevitability (and acceptability) of differences so they can differentiate from each other comfortably, stay connected, and practice talking in ways that haven't been possible for a long time, if ever. Phase three: We help them explore the meaning of apology and forgiveness, give them the opportunity to engage in both, and set the stage for them to support each other in healing emotional wounds that predate their relationship.

The third section explains how patterns of autonomic reactivity underlie the compulsive behaviors at the core of a couple's relational dynamics and illustrates how to discuss these phenomena with couples.

Finally, the book's fourth section describes some common challenges for couple therapists, while the fifth section provides additional experiential exercises so partners can rescript and repair conflictual interactions.

Because the IFIO approach is best grasped experientially, we recommend that therapists try these exercises personally before using them with clients. Try them with a partner, friend, or colleague. Alternatively, try them in your mind's eye with your own polarized parts, with someone you know, or with a couple you find manageable.

1 | Basic Concepts

PARTS

Intimacy from the Inside Out (IFIO) is built on the conceptual foundations of Internal Family Systems (IFS), a therapy developed by Richard C. Schwartz that endorses the normality of psychic multiplicity and engages the plural mind. IFS applies the systems thinking of family therapy to individual, couple, and group therapy. The basic premise of IFS is that we all have what Schwartz calls *parts*, as illustrated in common thoughts like "One part of me wants to go to the party; another part wants to stay home." Parts manifest in a developmental sequence throughout life, with their own personalities, temperaments, and a full range of feelings. We can notice the feelings, thoughts, and sensations of our parts, and we can talk to our parts. If we ask about their motives, they generally answer. Most vitally, regardless of their behavior, our parts want for us what we want: connection, validation, and love.

Like people, parts live in an inner community, where they develop alliances and get into conflicts. When this community's most vulnerable members feel scared, unlovable, or ashamed, other parts take on protective roles and try vigorously to do two things: banish the wounded part (the *exile*) from awareness and ensure that the injury never happens again.

We call proactive protectors *managers* and reactive protectors *firefighters*. Managers are the parts who focus on maintaining social connections and aim to conceal qualities they associate with weakness or badness. Their main tool is inhibition, which comes in many forms, including symptoms of mental distress like dissociation or denial; self-directed criticism, warnings, or threats; and bleak views of possibility. Looking for relief from emotional pain, reactive protectors respond to all this inhibition with rebellion and disinhibition. Provided their strategy works quickly, these parts don't concern themselves with consequences. Popular firefighter options include substance use, eating disorders, pornography, promiscuity, and other high-risk, high-engagement behaviors that offer good distraction. Although some inhibit and some disinhibit, all protectors aim to keep emotional pain out of awareness and don't understand that banishing vulnerable parts increases their panic and pain. When exiled parts panic and manage to break into awareness, protectors simply double down on excluding them. This repetitive, draining dynamic consumes a great deal of mental and emotional energy.

Life does not have to be a ping-pong match between inhibition and disinhibition. In addition to parts, we all have an inborn fount of compassion, spacious awareness, and wisdom—a seat of consciousness—of which most clients are not much aware: the Self. To fashion secure, stable attachment inside and out, partners in IFIO couple therapy practice unblending from protective parts and accessing their Self so they can heal wounds, personal and relational. Some experience the embodied Self as an inner spaciousness and calm; many describe it as an unusual alertness, a tingling energy running through their body and the sense of an open heart. The best way to understand this phenomenon is experientially. For illustrations of the Self and opportunities to access your Self with the exercises we provide, read on.

THE NATURE OF PARTS

Parts in general:

- Come into existence in a developmental sequence.
- Belong to an internal system of parts and contain a subsystem of parts, which in turn contains a subsystem of parts, ad infinitum.
- Have feelings, thoughts, opinions, and roles within their community.
- Have interests, gifts, talents, and skills.
- Have a positive intention for us.

Parts who *"are"*:

- Some parts get rejected for what they are (i.e., for being vulnerable) and live in a state of exile.

Parts who *"do"*:

- These parts take on protective roles and exile vulnerable parts in an effort to be safe:
  o Proactive protectors ward off emotional pain proactively. Their style is inhibitory, managerial, and socially acceptable.
  o Reactive protectors distract from emotional pain reactively. Their style is disinhibited, impulsive, and socially challenging.

UNBLENDING

The IFS therapist helps parts differentiate (or *unblend*) from the Self. The IFIO couple therapist helps partners differentiate from each other and helps parts differentiate from the Self. The experience of differentiating, or unblending, is like putting on a pair of much-needed distance glasses. When a part separates, we can suddenly see farther and with greater clarity. We can see the perspectives of more than one part and more than one person; we can see patterns and options.

In IFIO, we particularly want couples to appreciate how their pattern of protection (the defensive strategies of protective parts) and their vulnerability always go together. Underneath every protector and every conflict between protectors, we find exiled emotional pain. Protectors are not eager to reveal this pain. In fact, it's their job not to reveal it. But by being curious, we can coax them to become more communicative; by honoring their motives, we can get them to take us seriously; and by being kind, we can summon them closer. Curiosity, validation, kindness, and absolution for any damage they may have caused encourage protective parts to unblend and communicate directly about their concerns and fears so that we can help them.

To find parts, we look first to the body, going inside to notice sensations, feelings, or thoughts. Attention is our calling card. By picking a target and focusing on it, we invite it to pay attention to us, which is the beginning of a relationship. Because managers are inhibitory, they often show up in the joints, diaphragm, throat, jaw, shoulders, and lower back. Firefighters, who activate the endocrine and the nervous systems, can be found in fight-or-flight responses, like an increased heart rate, rapid breathing, and dilated pupils. Meanwhile, exiles are often in or around the heart, gut, or back (Schwartz & Sweezy, 2019). After noticing where and how a part shows up in the body, we ask permission to get to know it. Sometimes other parts object, especially if they are afraid of the target part. For example, some parts are explosively angry with other people or harshly critical internally. Throughout this manual, we will illustrate options for proceeding in cases like this.

But if it's okay to proceed, we start the interview by helping the target part (and all other parts) unblend so the client's Self can embody. If a part is not yet ready to unblend, one option is to go in the other direction and talk with it directly while the client listens. We can also invite a part to embody fully and show us what it feels or wants to do. As we interview protectors at the outset of therapy, we want them to know that they can get more of what they hope for by doing less. We tell the couple that their protectors are like loyal soldiers tasked with saving vulnerable young children. We want the partners to see their behavior in a historical context and soften toward them. We want their protectors to soften too.

While some individuals are quick to trust the therapist and experiment with unblending, others need a lot of reassurance. The protectors of both partners commonly need to know that (1) asking them to unblend is not an attempt to reject or silence them, (2) the therapist believes both partners have the strength and wisdom to take care of their own exiles, and (3) the therapist will support both partners at all times, even in moments of extreme reactivity. We reassure them on these points by giving them the opportunity to air their concerns. If a part will not unblend, we address its fears thoroughly and proceed only when it's ready. The following three questions, which we illustrate throughout the examples to come, elicit protector concerns about unblending:

1. To the client: "Does any part of you object to us paying attention to the target part?"
2. Directly to a protective part: "Are you willing to soften and separate just a little? You can always go right back to the way things are now if you want to."
3. To the client when protectors have unblended: "How do you feel toward [the target part]?"

PROJECTION IN RELATIONSHIPS

Protectors have an arsenal of behaviors at their disposal. They use our body, emotions, awareness, and behavior to achieve their goals. One such behavior, which Freud called *projection*, is particularly important in relationships. Projection goes one step beyond denying or distracting from emotional pain by extending an internal process to external relationships. In the process of projection, a protector in Person A criticizes Person B for displaying an attribute that is actually characteristic of another part of Person A—either an exile or another protector—who is being disowned. Protectors can project anything. It might be an intensely negative feeling like fear or anger, a vulnerable state like innocence, an inhibitory behavior like judging, an inhibited behavior like withdrawing or dodging conflict, or a disinhibited behavior like drinking too much or anxiously pursuing a partner. The projection may or may not be accurate for Person B, but it is always accurate for some part of Person A. Like all protective measures, projection is a way of managing vulnerability.

Although projection is central to much interpersonal conflict, couples tend to resist the concept. As a result, it works best to help them reclaim their projections experientially. We have a wide variety of exercises that revolve around a technique Schwartz named the *U-turn* (Schwartz & Sweezy, 2019). U-turn exercises reverse projection by asking partners to look inside for the driving force behind their conflict. Each exercise guides partners to attend internally, notice what their parts are feeling and saying, and inquire about their motives. U-turn exercises invariably reveal the old injuries (exiles) and long-held beliefs regarding safety that fuel protective reactivity. By doing a U-turn, each partner has the opportunity to witness the other tracing their feelings and behavior from protective reactivity back to exiled vulnerability. Moments of connection around painful early experiences open the door for a relational *re-turn* that is replete with compassion, empathy, and understanding.

AFFECT REGULATION AND THE U-TURN

The term *affect regulation* describes an individual's ability to modulate strong emotional states and stay present. This skill is critical for couples. Having the faculty to pause, make a U-turn, and unblend from intense reactivity lays the groundwork for self-soothing and returning to calm connection during or following a difficult interpersonal interaction. Because the U-turn is so important for couples, IFIO clinicians have developed a variety of U-turn questions, which are included in exercises and illustrated in many case examples.

THE U-TURN

- Notice reactivity, thoughts, feelings, and sensations.
- Inquire about what the reactive part *does* and *says* inside.
- Invite the reactive partner to:
  o Go inside and be curious.
  o Ask the part to unblend.
  o Ask who it is and who it protects.
  o Listen and validate.
- Invite the partner who said or did something triggering to do a U-turn too. The U-turn will reveal what was going on for them internally prior to making the triggering statement or doing the behavior.

IN-SIGHT AND DIRECT ACCESS

In IFS, we want parts to unblend so the Self can show up. With at least some measure of unblending, the client can be in communication with their parts from their Self. We say be "in communication" rather than "talk to" because only some people have verbal communication with their parts. Others see their parts or feel them kinesthetically, and some people experience parts in a combination of ways. The form of communication makes no difference because all options are possible internally. Any open channel between the Self and a part will serve. When the client communes with a part, we call it *in-sight*. However, when the client's parts won't unblend and no inner channel of communication is open, we need another option. Our second option, called *direct access*, involves the therapist talking directly with the client's parts. Direct access gets a lot of use in couple therapy, especially in the beginning.

In contrast to in-sight, direct access must be verbal. The therapist's Self talks to the client's part, while the client's Self (who has not yet been invited to participate) eavesdrops on the conversation. There are two kinds of direct access: explicit and implicit. In explicit direct access, the therapist names the blended part and asks for permission to speak to it directly ("I hear this part has something important to say but is not yet ready to make room for you. How about if I talk to it while you listen?"). Direct access gives the part an opportunity to be forthcoming about its concerns. In our experience, most clients do give permission for direct access, after which we can speak with the part about the client in the third person ("What do you do for Jane? What are you concerned would happen to Jane if you stopped doing that?").

Implicit direct access is different. Here the therapist simply talks with the blended protector without naming it as a part and without asking it what it does for the client ("I hear you're feeling really angry right now. Would you be willing to say more about that?"). This looks more like traditional talk therapy but differs in that the therapist knows they are talking to a part. Implicit direct access is a good way to begin if a part rejects parts language or objects to the idea that it is a part. In IFIO, we jump to using implicit direct access often and quickly to validate a protector's feelings and offer help, particularly when partners are caught in a loop of reaction and counterreaction and the autonomic nervous system (ANS) is activated. We help protectors calm down by validating their feelings, which, in turn, helps the rest of the internal system calm down.

We can't emphasize enough that getting into power struggles with protectors dependably ensures they won't give an inch. If you want extreme protectors to unblend, befriend them and stay curious ("Does this part have more to say?" or "Does it need anything from you or me right now?"). In addition, since protectors are motivated by fear, they need to know that the therapist has heard their fears and has a reasonable way of addressing them ("I hear your concern. It makes sense. Would you like us to slow down and hear more?"). For more on befriending parts, see *Internal Family Systems Skills Training Manual: Trauma-Informed Treatment for Anxiety, Depression, PTSD & Substance Abuse* (Anderson, Sweezy, & Schwartz, 2017).

UNBURDENING

Once partners are able to reliably unblend from protective parts and the Self is more available, we can begin the process of *witnessing* past traumas and helping exiles to *unburden*, or let go of self-defeating beliefs and unrelentingly extreme feelings (e.g., "Something is wrong with me," "I'm weak," "I'm too scared," "I'm worthless," "I'm unlovable," "I'm bad"), which were generated when the internal system believed that shameful personal qualities were the cause of someone else being critical. Exiled parts often carry a variety of burdens, which they will only release if they—and their protectors—feel safe and well connected with the Self. Once these conditions are met and exiles let go of their burdens, protectors can let go of their jobs and do something else.

In IFIO couple therapy, we foster a specific kind of unburdening: *relational unburdening*. As both partners unblend from their protectors and hold each other emotionally, they can take turns revisiting traumatic childhood events. Deep dives into relational trauma from childhood in which both partners' exiles share an emotionally corrective experience give couples a profound sense of connection and renewal.

TRANSFERENCE AND COUNTERTRANSFERENCE

Transference and countertransference can emerge at any time in therapy. From a parts perspective, these phenomena occur when parts—either the therapist's or the client's—respond to present-moment experiences as if the present were the past. They do this because the exile they protect is stuck in a kind of Groundhog Day existence in the past. By helping the exile who is stuck in this way, the client's Self corrects the distorted views of protectors (Schwartz & Sweezy, 2019). In our view, clients and therapists are in a parallel process, so countertransference calls for exactly the same attention to protectors and exiles as transference.

TIPS ON COUNTERTRANSFERENCE

Know your history and check yourself routinely:

- Am I siding with one partner?
- Do I feel friendly toward both?
- Does one partner scare or intimidate me? If yes, what do I do or say in response?
- Do I stay relaxed and regulated when a session becomes intense or their parts react to me?
- Which of their protectors is more challenging?
- Does my system up-regulate or down-regulate in response?
- What is my knee-jerk reaction? What is my first impulse?
- What do my protectors say about the couple? What do my exiles say?
- What was my role in my family (e.g., I tried to protect my siblings from my angry father)? Are there times I default to this role with my clients? If so, what is this part trying to do for me in those moments?

RELATIONAL NEUROBIOLOGY

Research in the field of neurobiology tells us that the ANS can reshape itself (Porges, 2007), which means couples who are entrenched in repetitive patterns of fighting and disconnection because of early relational trauma can change. In IFIO, we explain to couples—using simple, comprehensible terms—that neurobiology underlies behaviors that feel compulsive to them, and their neurobiology is plastic and will change as they practice new behaviors.

In the neurobiology section, we review relevant concepts and offer ideas for employing them in the context of IFIO. In our view, these concepts help couples heal and grow in several ways, including by:

1. Decreasing self-condemnation and partner-blaming while increasing partners' knowledge about how the brain and the ANS affect their ability to stay safely connected.

2. Helping partners stay present with themselves and each other as they learn to modulate the ANS and soothe distress in the body and mind.

3. Illustrating how the team approach to regulating the ANS—which we call co-regulation—is a powerful path to feeling safe and connected at any stage of life.

SUMMARY

In IFIO couple therapy, we aim for partners to experience a slew of benefits that come with thinking in terms of parts. First, the therapy can bypass the repetitive prologue of parts who spend time in therapy explaining, justifying, rationalizing, criticizing, or disowning problematic protective behaviors. Second, by thinking in parts and seeing their faults and imperfections as just one small part of a robust, vital, and larger whole, clients can challenge paralyzing global judgments like "I'm worthless." Third, when a client is able to feel curious about a firefighter's motives, they discover the real problem—the underlying one of vulnerability and emotional pain—and have the (often new) experience of feeling grateful to their firefighter. Fourth, by validating that they needed protection in the past and by being kind to the firefighter parts who provided that protection, partners gradually earn the kind of influence with their firefighters that manager parts can only dream of. Finally, as protectors unblend, partners gain the courage to open their hearts in their relationship.

GLOSSARY OF TERMS AND CONCEPTS

Like all psychotherapies, IFS and IFIO assign unique meanings to certain words and phrases. Here is a glossary of the language we use in this manual:

- **The 8 C's:** The qualities that characterize the Self: curiosity, calm, confidence, courage, connectedness, creativity, clarity, and compassion.

- **Blended:** A part is merged with another part or with the seat of consciousness, the Self. Blending occurs on a continuum such that the individual may be empathic and *feel with* a part, be substantially in agreement with a part, or go to the extreme of seeing the world entirely through the eyes of that part ("This *is* me!").

- **Burdened:** A part carries a burden. Painful beliefs to which parts adhere, extreme feelings state in which parts feel stuck, and recurrent distressing physical sensations that occur without narrative context, which turn out to symbolize or reenact aspects of past trauma.

- **Burdens:** Persistent negative, self-referential beliefs (e.g., "I'm unlovable," "I'm worthless"); recurring intense, trauma-related feeling states (e.g., terror, shamefulness, rage); and repetitious physical sensations that are frightening or painful.

- **Direct Access:** One of two principal methods used in IFS to communicate with parts. When a protector will not separate, or *unblend*, the therapist can speak directly to the client's parts, hence the term *direct access*. In direct access, the therapist may either speak to a part explicitly (e.g., "Can I talk to this part directly? Why do you want Pete to drink?"), or the therapist may use direct access implicitly, without stating that they are talking to a part. Direct access is the usual method to use with children (Krause, 2013) and is often used in IFIO couple therapy.

- **Do-Over:** An exiled part is stuck in the past and takes the client's Self back to that time and place where it instructs the Self to do whatever the part needed someone to do for it at the time. When that is complete, the Self brings the part out of the past and into the present.

- **In-Sight:** A form of internal communication between parts and the Self, which is the approach adults often use to communicate with and understand their parts. Internal communication requires the client to be aware of their parts—visually, kinesthetically, or aurally—and to have enough Self-energy to communicate with them directly. When protectors block internal communication, we use direct access instead.

- **Parts:** Internal entities, or subpersonalities, who function independently and have a full range of feelings, thoughts, beliefs and sensations. These entities, who also display Self-energy when they feel understood and appreciated, vary in appearance, age, gender, talent, and interests. They exist within the internal system where they take on various roles. When they are not exiled by other parts for their vulnerability and are not in conflict with each other over how to manage exiled parts, they contribute in a variety of ways to our wellbeing.

IFS classifies parts in three broad categories according to their role in the internal system. Injured parts (or exiles) who feel shameful exert a primary influence on other parts. Orbiting around *exiles* are two different categories of protective parts. Some protectors are proactive, aiming to ward off exiled vulnerability and further injury. We call them *managers*. Other protectors are reactive. They take on the job of distracting from and suppressing emotional pain when it breaks through despite the best efforts of our managers. We call them *firefighters*.

  1. **Exiles:** Revealed in feelings, beliefs, sensations, and actions, these parts have been shamed, dismissed, abused, or neglected in childhood and are subsequently banished by protectors, both for their safety and to keep them from overwhelming the internal system with emotional pain. A great deal of internal energy is expended by protectors keeping exiles out of awareness.

  2. **Proactive protectors (managers):** Managers focus on learning, functioning, and being prepared and stable. They are vigilant in trying to prevent exiles from flooding the internal system with emotional pain. In the service of keeping us task-oriented and impervious to pain, they have some standard tactics, including pragmatism, thinking, criticizing, and shaming.

  3. **Reactive protectors (firefighters):** Firefighters also aim to ward off emotional pain. However, they are the emergency response team, deployed *after* the memories and emotions of exiles break through to awareness despite the repressive, inhibitory efforts of managers. Reactive protectors use extreme measures that managers abhor, like alcohol and drug abuse, binge eating, excessive shopping, promiscuity, cutting, suicide, and even homicide. They are fiercely loyal to the mission of distracting from emotional pain and do not respond well when others try to control them.

- **Polarization:** Protectors routinely get into disagreements over how to manage emotional pain and end up in adversarial relationships. Over time, their conflicts become increasingly extreme and costly. However, when we acknowledge the good intentions and contributions of each part, they generally become willing to try something new. Once they witness the exile being healed by its relationship with the Self, they are able to let go of their protective jobs and choose a preferred role.

- **Self:** The seat of consciousness, an innate presence in each of us that brings balance and harmony to inner and outer systems by way of its nonjudgmental, transformative qualities, including curiosity, caring, creativity, courage, calmness, connectedness, clarity, compassion, presence, patience, persistence, perspective, and playfulness. While parts can blend with (i.e., overwhelm and obscure) the Self, the Self cannot be harmed and is available as soon as parts separate, or unblend.

- **Self-Energy:** The qualities of patience, curiosity, persistence, playfulness, loving-kindness, and compassion that the Self brings to its relationship with parts.

- **Self-Led:** This occurs when an individual has the capacity to hear, understand, and be present with parts internally and with other people externally, offering the clarity of a systemic perspective, a willingness to take responsibility, and the spirit of loving-kindness.

- **The Invitation for an Unburdened Exile:** After unburdening, the part can invite any quality of its own choosing to fill the space formerly occupied by the burden.

- **The Unburdening Process:** Taken as a whole, the unburdening process includes the Self witnessing the exile, the Self going into the past to help the exile in traumatic situations in whatever way it needs, the Self retrieving the exile from the past, the exile letting go of its burdens (unburdening), the exile inviting new qualities, and, finally, the Self checking in with protectors to see if they are ready to unburden and change roles.

- **Unblended (differentiated or separated from parts):** In this "being-with" experience, the Self is present and available to accompany parts empathically (feel with them), understand their experiences, and have compassion for (care about) them. When parts remain unblended and separate from the Self, not vying to dominate consciousness, we have access to our Self. The unblended state of being often translates into a sense of internal spaciousness.

- **Unburdening:** The moment when a burdened part lets go of burdens (intense, painful physical sensations; extreme emotions; harsh beliefs). This moment is often ceremonial and involves releasing the burden to one of the elements (light, earth, air, water, or fire) as in shamanic traditions. But an unburdening can also be spontaneous (Geib, 2016).

- **Witnessing:** The process by which a part shows and/or tells the client's Self about its experiences until it feels understood, accepted, loved, and self-accepting.

SECTION 2 | Treatment in Three Phases

This section describes and illustrates the three phases of treatment in IFIO and provides exercises for couples to use in session or at home. In the first phase, we get to know the couple, introduce the model, settle on goals, and offer hope. In the second phase, which covers most of the therapy, we challenge each partner's protectors kindly and firmly, track the circular nature of their conflict, and invite protectors to unblend so they can try something new to increase their choices and decrease their reactivity.

In the second phase of treatment, we give partners a relational perspective on shame and guide them through various U-turn explorations. If they ask for help with a specific rupture at the outset of therapy, we introduce our method for working with betrayal; otherwise we address betrayals as therapy progresses. As they master unblending and are able to stay emotionally regulated and curious for significant portions of a session, we introduce them to *courageous communication*, a way of speaking and listening without attacking or collapsing. Finally, if the timing is right, we invite one partner to do some individual work while the other acts as a witness.

This second phase is governed by two equally potent forces: (1) the couple's underlying pull to reconnect, which motivates them to keep engaging and (2) and their emotional eddies, which guide us to dive in where the flow is blocked (Herbine-Blank et al., 2016). Throughout all the various strategies we introduce—including tracking, unblending, the U-turn, courageous communication, and individual explorations—we invite the couple to step back, observe process over content, and discover how unmet needs incite protectors. The process is not linear. We come prepared with a view of the mind as a community that handles emotional injury by exiling its most vulnerable members and instituting a variety of protective strategies. On the basis of this model, we predict that protective parts will feel hopeless and frustrated at the outset of therapy.

Even so, we don't know how the couple will behave at any given moment. While the social arrangements of parts are predictable, individuals are full of surprises and every couple is unique. As a result, the therapist must be on their toes. Our job is to be open and creative. If a therapy seems stuck and unproductive, we check on ourselves first. If we notice countertransference feelings, we help our parts. What's hard in any given therapy is what's hard for us. If our parts are phobic about anger because our parents quarreled in our childhood, then we need to help our parts. As we go back and forth between tracking conflict, helping protectors unblend, helping partners do a U-turn, facilitating courageous communication, and diving in with one partner's exiles, we continually monitor the needs of our own inner community.

In the third phase, we come to repair, forgiveness, reconciliation, and the future. By this time, couples are clear about their parts, their partner, and their relationship, and they are less reactive with each other. Their intimacy is deeper, and it's time for them to envision their future. If the therapist has not already initiated a conversation about apology and forgiveness, this is the time. We support partners in exploring obstacles to apology and forgiveness, facilitate authentic repair, and help them share responsibility for the health of their relationship. When couples have more safety and trust, they can design a future based on new ways of thinking, feeling, and being.

THE THREE PHASES OF IFIO COUPLE THERAPY

Phase 1: Learning

- Meet the couple to assess their level of differentiation.
- Learn what they fear.
- Learn their emotional needs, hopes, and intentions for therapy.
- Offer possibilities.

Phase 2: Getting to the Heart of the Matter

- Teach the couple new communication skills to help them unblend and regulate their ANS.
- Get permission to be their *parts detector.*
- Track how they fight and how they're vulnerable, including:
  - How they negotiate needs
  - How they shame each other
  - How they receive shaming (i.e., how their protectors shame them)
- Walk the couple through the new communication behaviors you want them to learn.
- Get them in their bodies and deepen their work with experiential exercises.
- Promote and reinforce relational unburdening.
- Do individual work, including:
  - Unblending
  - Unburdening shamefulness
  - Having the partner as a witness
  - Practicing new communication skills
  - Returning to relational needs
  - Practicing skills that are more likely to get needs met

Phase 3: Ending

- Help the couple see each other as a resource rather than as the "wounder" or the "healer."
- Heal betrayals by guiding them in the process of repair and forgiveness.
- Provide support and guide partners as they gradually unblend and (if they decide to move forward together) develop a relationship based on acknowledging differences as well as sharing a vision.

PHASE 1 OF TREATMENT: LEARNING

Assessment: IFIO is Collaborative and Non-Pathologizing

Assessments in psychotherapy are often structured around diagnosing pathology. In IFIO, as in IFS, we don't categorize clients by diagnosis. In our view, the human mind consists of an internal system of parts and an undamaged Self. That internal system, like human systems at all levels, organizes itself to protect vulnerability—and does so with brilliance and creativity. But ultimately, parts do not have the resources to navigate a dangerous world alone; they need the Self and we aim to introduce them.

We begin therapy with interest and curiosity, meeting and greeting the couple's parts, learning about the beliefs and priorities of each partner's system, and getting a look at the system they've created together. In many cases, the couple's protectors will be blaming each other, and they will be stuck in a painful, self-absorbed "I" state that feeds on disconnection. Our goal, which we convey early on, is to help them reclaim their "we" state. After connecting with both partners, we communicate a few important facts about our role and the stance of the IFIO therapist:

1. We are not afraid of their parts.
2. We prioritize the safety of both partners.
3. We don't choose sides in disagreements.
4. We are open and curious about each partner's perspective.
5. We hold both partners with respect and curiosity, recognizing the validity of their experience and the vulnerability that drives their protective parts to extremes.

Ask Initial Questions, Listen, and Observe

To get a feel for the state of any given couple, we ask questions like:

- Why are you here?
- How do you feel about being different from each other?
- What do you hope for in your relationship?
- What do you wish to achieve in therapy?
- What do you fear most?

As we listen, we have the opportunity to gauge how differentiated they are from each other; to notice how differentiated their parts seem to be internally; to appraise the roles and relationships of their parts, inside and out; to estimate their baseline level of ANS dysregulation; to track and reflect back what each says accurately to anchor their narrative in our mind and help them feel safe; and to validate their feelings, large and small.

We also ask questions about their histories. Have they had a problem with: (1) mental illness, (2) drug or alcohol abuse, (3) their family of origin, (4) children and parenting, (5) sexuality, (6) betrayal, (7) cultural differences, (8) prejudice and bias in their larger context, (9) past therapy, or (10) apologizing and forgiving? This inquiry, which could last several sessions, gives us information that may prove relevant as therapy unfolds.

Introducing the IFIO Model

Depending on a couple's needs, IFIO can be introduced by talking about it or by diving in experientially and showing how it works. Regardless of how we choose to introduce the IFIO concepts, we include the following messages:

- All human beings possess *parts* and an undamaged *Self*.
- No single feeling or experience represents all of who we are at any given moment; parts are aspects of a larger whole.
- Some parts take on protective roles to ward off vulnerability, other parts are vulnerable, and still other parts have not been affected by wounding.
- IFIO is collaborative: our contract with you depends on your wishes and desires, which may change during therapy.
- You are free to confront, ask questions, disagree, and express yourselves continually. Our motto is "all parts of you are welcome." Your parts may need time to trust this invitation.
- We will start by understanding the parts who get caught in painful relational tangles.

AN INITIAL SESSION

Avi and Hannah were a cisgendered, heterosexual, European-American couple in their late thirties. They had been together, not married, for eight years total and had lived in New York City for three years. In addition to having many values in common, both were successful visual artists.

Their relationship had been very passionate until Hannah told Avi that she was ready to be married and have children. Avi responded that he was unsure about making a lifetime commitment. As their conversations about getting married became increasingly fraught and painful, they agreed they were at an impasse and sought therapy.

Therapist: Welcome. We spoke briefly about what's going on, but I want to start today by hearing more from you both. I'd like to know what's happening, what you wish for in therapy, and how I can help.

> *Inviting, listening, and observing*

Avi: Clearly, I'm the problem. [*looking at Hannah*] I know you want to get married. We always said we would. And do the baby thing. Now I'm not sure.

Therapist: You've been together for eight years. It sounds as if you have made some assumptions about where your relationship was headed, but now you, Avi, aren't sure.

Avi: [*nods*] That's the short of it.

Therapist: And I hear you have a part who thinks you're the problem.

> *Introducing parts language*

Avi: Well, Hannah thinks that.

Hannah: Yes, I do actually. It's not that he's the problem per se, but something's up all of a sudden. One minute we're on the same page, and the next he's all squirrelly about commitment. I don't get it. I'm upset, angry, and afraid.

Therapist: Can you say more about your fear?

> *Inviting vulnerability*

Hannah: I'm 35. If I'm going to have babies, I need to start yesterday. I love Avi. We have a great life. I would be devastated if our relationship ended.

Therapist: You make sense to me. From what you're saying, Hannah, this change in Avi is sudden, confusing, and scary?

Hannah: Yes. I feel sick just talking about it.

Therapist: And when the two of you try to talk about it, what happens?

Hannah: What happens, Avi?

Avi: I'm not sure. I freak out. I get panicky and feel this urge to run like hell.

Therapist: [*looking at Hannah*] And you?

Hannah: I get incredibly frustrated. I'm afraid he's going to run away, and I try to hold him in conversation. But I'm panicking too.

Therapist: I understand. Both of you have parts who freak out and panic. But you manage panic very differently. Am I right?

Hannah: That's true.

Therapist: [*addressing both*] Take a minute with my next question. What is the panic trying to communicate?

> *Offering a gentle invitation to inquire and listen internally*

Avi: [*after a moment*] I'm trapped.

Hannah: The opposite. I'm alone.

Therapist: This sounds very hard. I can see how and why you need help now.

> *Validating*

Hannah: I'm at the place where I need some answers and decisions.

Avi: Okay, so remember I mentioned feeling panicky? Well, here it is, right here in my throat.

Therapist: Can I help?

Avi: This sounds like an ultimatum. Yes, help would be great.

Therapist: Take a couple of deep breaths. [*pauses*] As strange as this next idea might seem, notice your throat and say "hi" to that feeling. Do you hear yourself saying any words to yourself?

> *Facilitating inner differentiation by noticing the feeling instead of being the feeling*

Avi: [*pauses*] No. This is a sensation.

Therapist: Okay. Sensations let you know that something important is happening. I can help you and Hannah unpack all this and figure it out. That may take some time, and if you do this, you will have a lot of feelings before we're finished. But we'll start by talking about the process of being in therapy. My guess is that no hard-and-fast decisions will be made today.

> *Offering help and fashioning containment for therapy*

Avi: Yeah, good. No decisions is good by me.

Therapist: Hannah, do you want to say anything?

Hannah: Wow! Just the thought of marrying me kicks off a panic attack? That hurts.

Avi: Hannah, it's not the thought of marrying you. It's the ultimatum that freaks me out.

Therapist: I'm getting the picture of what's happening with you both, and I know there is so much more to talk about. However, I have some information about the therapy process that I think will help. And I want to save time for questions about how I work, or about me in general.

Avi: Have you seen this before?

Therapist: I have, Avi. Many times.

Avi: And what happens?

Therapist: Everyone is different. This therapy will offer you both the safety to get curious about yourselves, to listen to each other and speak with each other differently, and to better understand what's happening. My experience tells me that once you have the capacity to stick with hard conversations without panicking, you will learn a lot more about each other, and the decisions you have to make will be easier.

Hannah: That would be good for me. I'm really in the dark here.

Therapist: I wonder if we can put decision making on hold until you've had the chance to do some exploring?

Hannah: That's a challenge for me.

Therapist: Let's listen to the part who just said it'll be a challenge and find out why.

Hannah: You think it's not all of me?

Therapist: Are you open to trying a little experiment with me to find out? Then I'll explain more.

Hannah: Okay.

Therapist: Stay with that sense of challenge for a minute. Where do you notice it?

Hannah: I hear these words in my head: *I need to know right now so I can deal with it.*

Therapist: So the voice in your head wants you to be prepared?

Hannah: Yes.

Therapist: And then what, Hannah?

Hannah: Then I can either relax or freak out.

Therapist: It wants to know the future?

Hannah: Exactly! I've been feeling so out of control.

Therapist: I hear you. As I said, if you work with me, we'll get to that. Right now, I will let you know how I work and what I believe is possible. How does that sound? [*they nod*] Avi, you mentioned on the phone that you know a little bit about IFS and have shared that with Hannah. I'm not going to give you a discourse on this method of couple therapy, which is based on IFS, but I think the basic ideas are worth understanding. In this model, we recognize that the minds of all human beings have a multitude of parts, or aspects of personality. That's normal. I, too, have parts. This explains why we can be feeling and thinking many different things at the same time. Are you with me so far? [*both nod*] What's nice about this for couples is realizing that one thought or feeling is never all of who you are. As you get to know your parts, you will understand yourself and each other better. For example, you have both been describing feeling defensive but also very vulnerable. We can find and help those different parts of you.

Hannah: Can you remind us what they are?

Therapist: I sure can. So you, Hannah, have described getting frustrated, a cousin of angry, right? To this way of thinking, you have a part who gets frustrated. You also described feeling afraid and uncertain. We would say that's a completely different part of you. One who feels much more vulnerable.

Hannah: Yes, they are different. One is strong and the other is weak.

Therapist: And you, Avi, said you get freaked out and scared. And then you want to run away. These are parts of you.

Avi: I understand what you're saying. This will take some time to get my head around, but I see what Hannah means. One part feels weak and one feels strong.

Therapist: The concept of parts can take time to grasp. It takes experience mostly. We could say one part feels protective and the other feels vulnerable. When these parts get caught up in your conversations, things get heated, and it's hard for you to slow down. Both of you are left feeling upset, is that right?

> *Emphasizing that some parts take on protective roles to ward off the vulnerability of other parts*

Avi: And then we feel really disconnected.

Hannah: And unsafe!

Therapist: That's right. Disconnected and unsafe. We don't have much time left today. I want you to go home and think about what we've discussed. If you decide to explore all this with me, I will gather more information about your histories, your families, and your hopes for therapy on an ongoing basis. In the meantime, I want you both to hear that I'm tracking what a painful time this is. And I hear that you could use help.

∼⌇↺

This is just one example of how an initial IFIO session might go. Every couple and every therapist are different. We encourage you to continue using any assessment tools you value and to find your own way of introducing the IFIO concepts while staying open, curious, and connected to the couple.

PHASE 2 OF TREATMENT: GETTING TO THE HEART OF THE MATTER

Tracking the Sequences of the Couple's Conflict

Salvador Minuchin, a family therapist in the late twentieth century, developed the strategy of *tracking* as a means of exploring negative interactions in families (Minuchin & Fishman, 1981). Similarly, IFIO therapists use tracking to assess a couple's predictable, repetitive, negative interactions.

Although couples often believe that one of them has "started" a fight and is to blame, we use the technique of tracking to shine light on process and move the conversation off the content of any given disagreement. While the couple's quarreling protectors want to discuss what happened this time and who's to blame, the relevant question is what happens every time they get into conflict and why their protective parts keep doing this regardless of content. To call attention to the feelings and needs underneath painful interactions, we not only unpack the couple's external, *inter*personal dynamics, we also unpack their internal, *intra*personal dynamics, which motivate protectors. As long as protectors keep activating over the course of therapy, we track their interactions.

TRACKING

- Differentiates parts from the Self
- Helps partners notice protector reactivity in the form of predictable sequences of negative interactions
- Reveals the feelings and needs of vulnerable parts, which fuel protective behavior
- Invites partners to try something new so they can experience a different outcome

---

To track a sequence effectively, we stick with the following roadmap. First, we listen carefully to the couple's interaction and get details about each partner's behavior ("What do you do or say to your partner?"). Although couples believe the content of their fight is important, we stick with tracking how they interact. Next, we interview protectors about their motives ("What is this part afraid would happen to you if it didn't get so angry on your behalf?" or "What does this part hope for?") to learn about their hopes, fears, and needs. Rather than telling people how they feel or what motivates their protectors, we invite a process of self-exploration.

Our motto is "Ask—don't tell." By exploring, we flesh out the cycle of their fights experientially and help them recognize the predictability and repetitive nature of their fights. In addition, we reflect back what we hear each partner saying and pay attention to their level of autonomic arousal. If it gets too high, we intervene.

Finally, we issue an invitation of possibility. That is, we invite partners to imagine being less reactive and having more choice in how they respond to each other:

- "What if, regardless of your partner's reaction, you could stay centered and speak for what you want and need?"
- "What if you were less reactive, friendlier, and felt you had more choices about how to respond in these important conversations?"
- "If we could do something together to help both of you to be less reactive, feel more empowered, and have more hopeful interactions, would you be interested?"
- "If I could help each of you have more choice in how you respond when you hit communication snags, would you be interested?"

While tracking the couple's interactions, we also present them with four U-turn questions that were designed to help them listen carefully inside and learn from their parts. These particular questions are a subset of the larger number of U-turn questions we illustrate throughout the manual. To help partners answer, we explain each question. (The explanations offered here were developed by IFIO trainer Kate Lingren.)

1. "When your partner does X, what happens inside you?"

   - Explanation: "Your reactivity comes from your vulnerability. If I can help each of you feel less vulnerable and less reactive, you will be aware that you have choices, both individually and together. Rather than focusing on your partner, I will help each of you focus inside, on your vulnerability and on how your parts try to stay safe. I will especially do this in the beginning of therapy."

2. "And then what do you notice in your body?"

   - Explanation: "I ask you to notice what's happening physically when your partner does X because that helps us locate reactive parts who need your help."

3. "What is your first impulse?"

   - Explanation: "I ask you to notice your first impulse because protective parts react to perceived threats by fleeing, fighting, or freezing. When you notice parts who react in one of these ways, they notice you. Noticing you is the first step a part can take to separate, or unblend, from you. As soon your parts unblend, you will feel more spacious, less pressured to respond quickly, better able to help them, and more curious about what other people are experiencing."

4. "What do you hear yourself saying to yourself about you, your partner, or this relationship?"

   - Explanation: "I ask what you hear yourself saying about yourself and other people because protective parts try to keep us safe by telling us stories. Though they mean well, their stories are usually colored by past experience and can seriously distort our view of the present. Our aim here is to befriend your storytelling parts and solve this underlying problem of feeling unsafe so they don't have to work so hard."

These questions help protectors who have intense feelings to unblend so partners can regulate their ANS and speak their truth without attacking or collapsing.

TRACKING PATTERNS OF CONFLICT

Jane and Doran were a cisgendered, lesbian, African-American couple in their mid fifties. They had been together for 18 years and married for 10. Jane had a teenage son with a previous partner who lived with them part time. But by choice they had no children together. Both were employed as health care practitioners.

The following dialogue between Jane and Doran illustrates how to track the sequence of a couple's conflict.

Jane: [*chuckles*] Maybe you can fix her today.

Doran: She may be joking, but she does think I need to be fixed. [*turning to Jane*] All I really want, Jane, is more time with you.

Jane: What do you mean? I spend a lot of time with you. But remember, I earn most of the money, and we're over our heads in debt.

Therapist: [*to Jane*] When Doran said, "I want more time with you," what happened inside you?

> *Asking a U-turn question that invites Jane to be curious about her reaction to Doran*

Jane: I guess I got defensive.

Therapist: I'm going to restate that as "A part of me got defensive," okay?

> *Sticking to parts language*

Jane: What difference does it make?

Therapist: I think it'll make a big difference, but let's try it out and you can tell me if I'm right.

> *Opting for showing rather than telling*

Jane: Okay. A part of me got defensive.

Therapist: What are you noticing in your body?

> *Anchoring the target part*

Jane: My chest is tight. I notice anger.

Therapist: And what do you hear yourself saying to yourself?

> *Helping the partners listen for vulnerability or projection*

Jane: I never get it right for her.

Therapist: Feeling you never get it right. I imagine this is hard or painful.

> *Validating and being curious about underlying feelings*

Jane: Yes, it is.

Therapist: It sounds to me like you feel angry and defensive. Any other feelings?

> *Making time for the client to continue to check inside*

Jane: [*pausing*] I feel hurt.

Therapist: I think I am hearing several parts. Let me see if I get this right. Angry, defensive, and hurt, and some part that says, "I can't get it right."

Reflecting, giving an overview, and checking again for agreement or disagreement

Jane: Yes, that's right.

Therapist: And when all this is happening inside you, what do you do or say to Doran?

Detailing behaviors

Jane: I just want to get out of there.

Therapist: And do you go away?

Jane: I notice I stay at work longer, or sometimes when I get home, I just go up to my office and get on the computer.

Therapist: It sounds like you withdraw.

Jane: I do.

Therapist: [*to Doran*] Are you aware of the part of Jane who withdraws?

Doran: I certainly am.

Therapist: And when Jane's parts are taking her away, what happens inside you?

Asking a U-turn question to invite curiosity

Doran: I hate to admit it, but I get angry and loud.

Jane: [*interrupts*] She gets critical.

Therapist: [*to Jane*] I'm going to ask you to wait so I can listen to Doran for a few minutes. Actually, I'm going to ask both of you to hold off on speaking while the other person is talking. Can we agree to that for now?

Contracting for safety

Jane: Okay, okay. It's hard.

Therapist: I understand how hard it is given where you are. Thank you for doing something hard.

Validating protective response while maintaining the boundary

Therapist: [*to Doran*] So you have a part who gets loud?

> *Sticking to parts language*

Doran: Yes, loud, and I hate to admit it, demanding.

Therapist: What happens in your body when you get loud and demanding? And what do you hear yourself saying to yourself?

> *Asking U-turn questions*

Doran: I have to admit that I hear myself wondering: *What's wrong with me? Why does Jane avoid me?*

Therapist: Are you aware of that part right now?

Doran: Yes, I have a lump in my stomach. I feel bad.

Therapist: Let's connect with it for a moment and find out more.

Doran: I don't like feeling this way.

Therapist: This makes a lot of sense to me, Doran. Just like Jane, it sounds like you have a couple of active parts in these interactions. One part gets loud and demanding and the other says: *What's wrong with me that Jane is avoiding me?* Am I getting that right?

> *Validating, mirroring, and checking for agreement*

Doran: Yes, you've got it.

Therapist: And it sounds like there might be a relationship between these two parts of you. The bigger that lump in your stomach gets, the louder and more demanding your frustrated part becomes? [*Doran nods*] Okay. I want to ask both of you a question. I'll start with you, Doran, to get a sense of this part who gets loud and demanding. What might happen if it didn't do that?

Doran: [*pausing*] I'd never get her attention. We'd stay disconnected and I'd never get my needs met.

Therapist: So, this part of you is trying to be connected with Jane?

Doran: Yes. I guess it is. But it doesn't really work, does it?

Therapist: [*to Jane*] Did you know this?

Jane: Of course not. I just feel criticized.

Therapist: And what about the part of you who withdraws. Are you aware of it right now?

Jane: I can still feel it, but I feel less guarded hearing what Doran just said.

Therapist: And what might that part be concerned about? What if it let you stay and not withdraw?

Jane: [*pausing*] I would just keep being criticized.

Therapist: And then what?

Jane: I would keep feeling misunderstood.

Therapist: And then what?

Jane: More hurt.

Therapist: I imagine the part who feels hurt would rather feel appreciated, like you are doing enough and being successful. I think that's what I heard. Am I right?

Jane: You're right!

Therapist: I want to reflect back what I'm hearing from both of you. This sounds like a dilemma related to needs. Jane, when Doran tries to have more time with you and her parts get loud and demanding, as she describes it, you have a part who feels hurt, like you can't get it right. Then you withdraw to protect yourself. And Doran, when Jane withdraws, you feel bad and disconnected, and then you try to get her attention by getting louder and more demanding to protect yourself. And it goes on like this, back and forth with each of you feeling more protected but less connected. Does this sound like the pattern?

> *Naming the sequence and the patterns of reaction and counterreaction*

Doran: It's the pattern for sure.

Jane: [*nods in agreement*] It feels hopeless. We're really stuck.

Therapist: I understand that this cycle causes you to feel hopeless, and you would break the pattern if you could. I have a question for you. If I could help each of you to have many more choices in how to respond when you feel reactive, would that be good? [*they nod*] And if you could understand what your protective parts are hoping for, would that be good? [*they nod*] And, finally, if I could help you shift this pattern of reaction and counterreaction, would you be interested?

> *Issuing the invitation of possibility*

Jane: I'm interested. How about you, Doran?

Doran: I would certainly be interested. I hate being at odds all the time.

۞

We want couples to slow down and focus on their process rather than the content of their disagreements. The following worksheet, **Who Am I in a Conflict?** is designed to help couples track their patterns of conflict. The more separation partners get from their protectors and the more they see how their protectors contribute to the problem, the more they understand the relationship of all this protection to their own vulnerability.

Client Worksheet

WHO AM I IN A CONFLICT?
THE SEQUENCE TRACKING WORKSHEET

Tracking sets the stage for a U-turn and reveals the protectors who engage in conflict. By becoming familiar with how they engage in arguments, you will, right away, begin the process of breaking uncomfortable patterns of fighting.

1. As you watched your partner say or do whatever it is that triggers your protectors, what did you notice?

   What happened in your body?

   _____

   _____

   What did you hear yourself saying to yourself?

   _____

   _____

   Were you aware of any feeling(s)? If so, which ones?

   _____

   _____

   What was your first impulse?

   _____

   _____

2. What did you do or say in relationship to that person?

   _____

   _____

3. What response did you get back?

   _____

   _____

Copyright © 2021, Toni Herbine-Blank, Martha Sweezy, *Internal Family Systems Couple Therapy Skills Manual*. All rights reserved.

4. How did you react to that?

_____

_____

5. What did you notice as you stepped back and allowed yourself to see this cycle of reaction and counterreaction?

_____

_____

6. What did you learn about:

Your protector's job or role?

_____

_____

Your protector's wish for you?

_____

_____

How long it has had this job?

_____

_____

What it fears about not responding in this way?

_____

_____

Who it protects?

_____

_____

7. How did your protector respond to your invitation to be in relationship with you in this moment?

_____

_____

Copyright © 2021, Toni Herbine-Blank, Martha Sweezy, *Internal Family Systems Couple Therapy Skills Manual*. All rights reserved.

Courageous Communication: Change Your Conversation to Change Your Relationship

Couples benefit from learning to speak and listen well. Brain science tells us that empathic communication rewires the brain (Siegel, 2007) and supports changes in patterned behavior. Empathic communication means "feeling with" someone else without getting overwhelmed by their feelings. When we empathize, we feel with—but we don't confuse ourselves with—the other person: "I can imagine what's happening for you and resonate with your feelings. Though I know I'm not you, I have these feelings sometimes too." When we feel compassion for someone else, we care and feel concerned. We want couples to be able to empathize with and feel compassion for each other. In IFIO, we help partners maintain a self-other distinction inside and out so they can empathize safely and feel compassion for each other. Feeling known and understood initiates a positive cycle of connection and caring because it feels so good.

That said, staying curious and open-minded while listening to someone who feels hurt and angry describe the impact of your behavior takes willingness and courage. Speaking and listening well, which both require physiological regulation, call for a level of skill and patience that many couples have not had the opportunity to cultivate. On the other side of the fence, speaking about the other's impact truthfully without attacking, collapsing, or panicking also takes courage. Good communication requires both partners to stay in the conversation until everyone feels heard and understood, but when protectors feel threatened by differences, they can behave in ways that are far from ideal.

For example, a protector may refuse to listen because it:

- Fears being infected by the other person's perspective
- Believes listening signals agreement
- Believes they will not be treated fairly and will not have a chance to rebut

Fearful protectors often:

- Move quickly to find a solution to the perceived problem
- Shut down the conversation by "agreeing to disagree"
- Stop listening and focus on formulating a counter-response because they believe listening signals agreement

In IFIO, we help partners tune in to their parts and help them unblend so they have the bandwidth to tune in to their partner and deepen their intimacy, both verbally and nonverbally. Listening is powerful, calming behavior. It invites the same treatment in return. Ironically, the parts who long to be heard also tend to be protected by parts who associate listening with being powerless and, therefore, refuse to listen. They are afraid of being influenced, controlled, humiliated, or never having the opportunity to be heard. Repetitive patterns of conflict, therefore, involve each partner having an ongoing inner experience of not listening carefully, which is linked to a history of not speaking skillfully.

Even as fighting couples accuse and injure each other, they are wondering, "Do you hear me? Am I safe with you? Will you meet my needs?" But they can't hear this in themselves because their protectors are busy looking outward, chanting, "*You* can't be trusted! *You* aren't safe! *You* won't meet my needs!" To get to those essential underlying questions, we first help protectors settle down. We start by asking them about their hopes and fears. We listen to them carefully. Wary protectors fear change, and angry protectors like the energy and power of righteous anger. We check for these parts proactively and listen to them carefully too. Once they feel heard, we can offer to help the parts they protect.

Although protective extremes undermine secure attachments and safety, keep in mind that this is not how protectors see it. They operate in a realm—the psyche—where time travel is the norm, and they may be spending more time in a dangerous past than in the present. For them, negative feelings in the present, like fear or shame, simply reinforce storylines from the past (e.g., "I'm being attacked!"). By reacting accordingly, they recreate the kinds of interactions they intended to prevent. In this way, protectors keep the past very much alive and active inside the partners who sit before us. While we honor their urgency and good intentions, we also help them stand down. In particular, we arrange for safe, respectful, and courageous communications by using the U-turn. As protectors stand down, couples gain confidence that they can differ safely and have difficult conversations productively, which, in turn, helps them find a more openhearted perspective on living and being in a relationship.

THE AIMS OF COURAGEOUS COMMUNICATION

- Promote unblending and co-regulation.
- Help the couple move safely from content to process.
- Help the protective system trust that a different way of communicating will bring relief.
- Invite vulnerable parts to be seen and heard.

After unblending, each partner practices returning from inner exploration to listen from their Self and speak for their parts. If partners are highly reactive and not well-differentiated internally, this process can be slow. But over time, the whole practice—self-examination, openhearted listening, and unblended speech—generates curiosity about the other person's experience, as well as a growing acceptance that there is no danger in having different perspectives. When protectors no longer believe that a partner's differences threaten their survival, dialogue becomes natural and comfortable.

IFIO's courageous communication borrows from the Imago Dialogue technique (Hendrix, 1988), which was designed to promote a feeling of safety and reveal childhood wounds under troubled interpersonal dynamics. The IFIO version of courageous communication, however, adds an inner dimension to the Imago process by cultivating relationships between each person's parts and their Self. With healthy inner differentiation and attachment, partners feel safer differentiating from each other and are better able to practice behaviors that create secure interpersonal attachment.

Courageous communication requires attuned listening and responsible self-disclosure. Listening *and* speaking skillfully are both necessary. No one can be present and attentive if their internal system is fighting, fleeing, or numbing. We help the person in the role of listener first by asking them to: (1) listen to their partner's experience without reacting, (2) wait before responding, and (3) consider the truth in what their partner is saying rather than disagreeing or engaging in self-attack. To help protectors and the ANS relax, we offer the listening partner ample time to express fears. We also invite them to interrupt and ask for help whenever they need.

COURAGEOUS COMMUNICATION: PART 1

Listening Skillfully

- Really listening (listening from the Self) when another person describes your impact can be a challenge and takes courage. We invite listeners to be aware that their partner's feedback is not an objective truth and that listening to their partner is an opportunity to learn something about their partner, themselves, and their relationship.

- Breathing deeply while listening helps. If the listener feels reactive, upset, angry, or vulnerable, they may choose to slow the process down and get help.

- It helps to remind clients that a more vulnerable part who has a need lies beneath their partner's reactive behavior. Are the listener's parts willing to relax so they can listen from the Self? Are they available?

- What is the listener hearing? Can they imagine that this feedback will be useful? Are they willing to ask themselves, *What about this rings true and what does not?*

- As they listen, are their parts willing to let them be curious first and speak for their parts with Self-energy after?

Next, we support the speaker by inviting their protectors to speak about their fears. Since protectors often try to get needs met by avoiding conflict, collapsing, manipulating, or bullying, the idea of speaking directly about needs can be a challenge. If they accept this invitation, they let go of power, which some protectors will resist. Threatened, blended protectors raise the speaker's autonomic arousal and set off their impulse to flee, shut down, or fight back (Cozolino, 2008). The speaker can't think or speak when they are in this state. Therefore, we have to help their protectors unblend before proceeding with courageous communication.

COURAGEOUS COMMUNICATION: PART 2

Speaking Skillfully

- In order to speak *for* activated parts *from* our Self, we have to be present and take time to understand our parts.

- This is an opportunity for the speaker to talk about their part's experience with another person. Essentially, they speak about what happens inside when they are relating with the other person. The speaker is not evaluating or criticizing their partner. Nor are they trying to help their partner improve, be more self-aware, or be a better person.

- The speaker should consider their goals before speaking. The way they speak (speaking for their parts) will help them speak skillfully and affect the outcome.

- The speaker should ask if their partner is available to listen before beginning.

- Remind the speaker that they will be speaking about their own experience, not an objective reality.

- Before the speaker speaks, they should check inside to determine if their system is ready to explore vulnerable feelings and needs. If the system is ready, they can speak for a need or a fear. If not, the therapist can help the speaker explore whatever concerns came up.

Appreciation and acknowledgment go far in helping angry protectors soften. In particular, threatened protectors are more willing to unblend when we listen carefully, validate their fears, and appreciate their role. It also helps to suggest an alternative to their current strategies for keeping things safe by offering ongoing help. Essentially, we are asking them to sacrifice their current positions for the long-term greater good of themselves and the system they protect, and they need to feel confident of the outcome.

HELPING AN ANGRY PROTECTOR UNBLEND

1. Validate the anger. Make eye contact, be compassionate, and be present. Speak to the protector directly:

    "Given that this is your experience…"

2. Validate and empathize with the underlying need. See the exiles beneath the rage.

    "Your need to be heard makes complete sense…"

3. Challenge the behavior and name the consequence.

    "This kind of communication will not get you what you hope for. Your partner will likely not hear you or be able to respond in the way you want them to."

4. Offer an alternative that includes your help.

    "Will you let me help you speak for your feelings and needs?"

ROADMAP FOR INTRODUCING COURAGEOUS COMMUNICATION

Step 1: Listen, track cycles, and invite the couple to talk about difficult issues in a different way (e.g., "Will you let me help you?").

Step 2: Contract to be their parts detector (e.g., "I am here to help you, so I will slow down or stop the interaction if parts begin to overwhelm").

Step 3: Invite the couple to negotiate who will speak and who will listen first.

Step 4: Help the listener prepare by noticing parts who might not want to listen. Encourage the listener to breathe and notice their heart. Help the listener unblend and be emotionally available.

Step 5: Coach the speaker to help their parts unblend and be spoken for. Encourage each partner to stay in relationship with their own parts (e.g., "What are you noticing in your body?"). Do not get caught in content or in helping them find solutions. You may need to ask one partner to wait while you help the other unblend and speak for their parts (e.g., "What is this part concerned would happen if it were to unblend and let you speak for it?"). Validate the experience and feelings of the parts of both partners. Confront protectors firmly and kindly.

Step 6: If appropriate, encourage the speaker to move toward speaking for vulnerable feelings or childhood wounding (e.g., "Are these feelings familiar? Is there something happening that reminds you of your childhood?").

Step 7: Help the listener respond from the heart with empathy. No part should be left hanging. Some questions and requests to use with the listener include:

- "Can you reflect the essence of what you just heard?"
- "Does any of this information make sense to you? In what way?"
- "What does your heart say?"

If the listener does not empathize with the speaker, offer empathy yourself. Examples of empathic statements include: "The essence of what I'm hearing is…" and "It makes perfect sense to me that…" It is important to meet the client's self-disclosure with understanding, mirroring, and acknowledgment. Otherwise, a response of deep shame is likely to follow—and perhaps a protective adaptive reaction (Siegel, 2003).

Step 8: Once the speaker has received an empathic response from the listener (or you), ask the listener to pay attention inside.

Step 9: Check back with the speaker. Have they received the response? Has it made an impact? Do the parts who have been spoken for feel understood? Is there anything more to say? The speaker may feel complete and have nothing further to add, or they may feel moved to respond.

Step 10: If there is time, have the listener and speaker switch roles. When switching, remind the couple about the respective jobs of the listener and speaker as needed. When both partners are ready, ask the one who was just listening to speak for their parts.

SETTING THE TABLE FOR A HARD CONVERSATION WITH COURAGEOUS COMMUNICATION

Mark and Mateo were cisgendered, European-American, gay men who had no children. At the outset of their relationship 15 years earlier, they had made an agreement that they could each have sexual activity outside their relationship if they practiced safe sex and did not withhold emotional or physical intimacy from each other. They had maintained this arrangement through 12 years of partnership and three years of marriage. Mateo had recently gone through a bout of cancer from which he had recovered completely. Mark had been supportive and available throughout treatment and recovery. Now they sought therapy specifically to improve communication and feel successful when having challenging conversations about sex. Their cycle tended to begin with reactive protectors flaring up and fighting to be heard. Mateo's subsequent response was to withdraw while Mark had a protector who pursued. When a conversation felt threatening, neither of them could regulate their nervous systems long enough to pause, recalibrate, and finish.

In the following dialogue, the therapist sets the table for a courageous conversation by using four U-turn questions. In general, U-turn questions orient partners to notice the feelings, needs, and desires of their parts, which helps their parts unblend. We ask these four U-turn questions at the outset of any conversation the couple has identified as potentially difficult.

Therapist: You've asked for help speaking and listening about your sexual relationship. I hear things are changing, and talking about it has been challenging.

Mateo: Agreed.

Mark: Yes.

Therapist: Before diving in, let's try a short experiment to sort out and understand your parts who have concerns about the conversation to come. Let's start by having both of you listen inside before you speak. As you listen inside and think about starting to talk about your sexual relationship, what parts do you notice?

> *The first U-turn question*

Mark: I feel anxious.

Therapist: How do you notice that in your body?

> *Checking for ANS activation and their level of blending*

Mark: My stomach is tight.

Therapist: Mateo?

Mateo: My stomach too. But I would say I feel more fear more than anxiety.

Therapist: Are you both available to speak for these feelings—these parts—with each other now?

Mateo: [*turning to Mark*] I am really scared about what it will mean if I'm honest. I'm changing. The cancer changed me. So many things are different, and I don't know what's going to happen. Even as I say this, I feel the fear getting bigger.

Therapist: Mateo, let's slow down and notice the fear. Where is it in your body?

Mateo: All over really. I have the urge to disappear.

Therapist: Can you say more?

Mateo: I guess it's a fear of being left… rejected.

Therapist: Does that make sense?

Mateo: It does.

Therapist: Great. Let the part know you get it. What does it need to feel your presence and not take over?

Mateo: [*after a few breaths*] It's actually okay. We've needed to have this conversation for a while. I feel scared, but I trust Mark, and I believe we'll get through it.

Mark: This is helpful. Slowing down rather than jumping in and failing. That's how we get into a gridlock.

Therapist: [*to Mark*] And your anxiety?

Mark: I'm afraid we'll want different things.

Therapist: And then what?

Mark: The relationship will suffer.

Therapist: And then?

Mark: Ultimately, we wouldn't stay together.

Therapist: And…

Mark: I don't want that.

Therapist: So what I'm hearing is that you both have parts who feel anxious about disconnection. Mateo, your parts fear rejection; and, Mark, yours fear the relationship ending. Am I getting this?

Mateo: You are.

Therapist: Does it make sense that talking about sex would be a challenge given all these concerns?

Mark: It makes more sense now.

Therapist: Okay. I have a second question for you both. You have not listened or spoken about this with each other fully. What has that cost you? Again, take a moment to listen inside. When you're ready, speak for the parts you notice.

The second U-turn question

Mark: What I hear inside is that I'm in the dark. I don't know what's up. I've avoided asking Mateo what's going on. I'm worried that I'm going to have to give something up and I'll feel angry, so I just don't say anything.

Therapist: What would be the worst thing about feeling angry?

Mark: Things never go well when I get angry.

Therapist: And the cost of not expressing what you feel?

Mark: Things build up and I get irritable.

Therapist: Thanks. [*turning to Mateo*] What feelings did you notice?

Mateo: Not an angry part but other feelings I'd rather not face.

Therapist: And the cost of not facing them?

Mateo: I just get on with whatever is in front of me, but the feelings do build up.

Therapist: How does not talking about your feelings impact your partner? How does it impact your relationship?

> *The third U-turn question*

Mark: Distance.

Mateo: Distance, avoidance, and superficial conversations.

Mark: Right.

Therapist: Disconnected?

Mark: Yes, disconnected.

Therapist: What are your intentions in having this conversation?

> *The fourth U-turn question*

Mateo: Well, I want to be heard and understood. And, ultimately, I want Mark to be okay and the relationship to be okay.

Mark: I want to understand Mateo, and I want the relationship to stay intact.

Therapist: The fear makes sense to me.

Mark: What I just heard myself say is *I don't know what's going on*. It would probably be useful to find out. So one of my goals is to listen without getting upset.

Mateo: I need to speak up. That's clear. I don't have much of a template for being visible. I was raised by my mother and grandmother—two very strong women, but they kept their mouths shut when they felt threatened. That was the rule.

Therapist: Okay. First, I'd like both of you to take another moment to check inside. Notice your breathing and any shifts in your physical experience, any impulses to fight or pull away.

> *Checking for ANS activation and their levels of blending*

Mateo: I feel more relaxed. Less afraid. I guess those threatened parts are giving me some space.

> *Verbalizing the experience of unblending*

Mark: I'm still anxious because I don't know what I'm going to hear. But less so.

Therapist: And what do you notice in your body? In your stomach?

Mark: More relaxed.

Therapist: Mateo, how's the urge to disappear?

Mateo: I feel more present than I have in a long time.

Therapist: Great. How do you think speaking and listening to each other would go from this place?

Mark: Much better. But I have no idea how to get to this place when we're on our own.

Therapist: Of course, you don't. And that's why we start slowly and practice unblending as we go. We help your parts relax so you can speak for what's going on with them and *respond* instead of *reacting* to each other. Shall we give it a try? [*both agree*]

Once clients have gone through these U-turn questions, their vigilant, concerned parts may be more willing to unblend, at which point the couple can have that courageous conversation, as Mark and Mateo do here.

Therapist: Mark, you said you felt available to listen to what's happening for Mateo. Is that still true?

Mark: It is.

Therapist: [*to Mateo*] And with my help, Mateo, are you ready to start the conversation?

Mateo: With your help? That sounds good. I can feel myself relaxing.

Therapist: [*to Mark*] Scan inside again and notice any parts who have any concerns about listening.

Mark: As I said, I have a part who is afraid Mateo is going to ask me to do something I don't want to do—make changes I'm not ready to make.

Therapist: So this part is worried you will have to do something you don't want to do?

Mark: Yes.

Therapist: What if, for today and perhaps the next couple of sessions, we take making requests and negotiating for needs off the table so we just can concentrate on really listening to each other?

Mateo: That's hard for us. We *really* like to get to the heart of the matter fast so we can figure out what to do.

Therapist: And what is the hope of your get-there-fast parts?

> Another U-turn question

Mateo: [*after a moment of silence*] The hope is we get a strategy that will work quickly so we—

Mark: [*interrupting*] So at least we both get something and don't fight.

Mateo: But eventually that leads back to what we were just talking about. We get nowhere or we fight anyway.

Therapist: Exactly! So what do you think about trying something different now? [*they nod*] Mark, check inside and see if you've got a genuine yes before Mateo speaks.

Mark: [*closes his eyes for a few seconds and then opens them*] Okay, Mateo, let's hear it! I really am interested.

Mateo: [*smiles*] I feel that.

Therapist: Before you speak, Mateo, let me remind you that you're speaking for your parts. For what you want Mark to understand about you right now. If it feels like either of you is getting taken over or flooded, I'll slow everything down to help you unblend. How does that sound?

Contracting to be a "parts detector"

Mateo: Good.

Mark: Great.

Therapist: Are you ready to speak, Mateo?

Mateo: Since my diagnosis and all that followed, something around sex has changed for me. My sex drive isn't the same. I'm rethinking who I am. I was so lucky. Not everyone with a cancer diagnosis survives and goes on like I have.

Mark: [*nods*] I've noticed.

Mateo: [*grimaces*] This is so awkward. Especially in front of a third person.

Therapist: Of course. Can you keep going?

Mateo: I'm really worried that these changes might affect our relationship in big ways—

Mark: [*interrupting*] In what big ways?

Therapist: Mark, what just happened?

Mark: Wow! It must have been that part who is afraid Mateo will ask me for something I can't give.

Therapist: Can you reassure it? Right now, you're just listening.

Mark: Okay, it's settling down. Sorry, Mateo.

Mateo: I'm not asking you for anything. I can barely figure myself out, let alone ask anything of you. I'm afraid, Mark. Afraid!

Therapist: Can you say more about this fear?

Mateo: I'm jumbled inside. I'm not sure.

  Therapist: Can we stay with the jumbled feeling for just a moment so you can get a little more information about it?

Mateo: [*closes his eyes and leans back*] In my head, this conversation was going to be about life and death and priorities changing. It still might be. But what I am aware of right now is feeling like damaged goods.

Mark: Oh God. [*grabbing Mateo's hand across the couch*] I'm so sorry you feel that way!

Mateo: [*tearing up*] I wonder if I'm ever going to feel healthy and strong—sexy, desirable—again.

  Therapist: Do you know the part who's speaking now, Mateo?

Mateo: I do.

  Therapist: And does it feel okay to keep speaking for it to Mark?

Mateo: [*looks at Mark and smiles*] He's sticking around. I guess I can keep speaking for him.

Mark: I'm available. I had no idea. I'm really listening.

(Co-regulation)

❧

Our job is to support partners in self-regulation and the couple in co-regulation. In this session, the therapist first used four U-turn questions to help Mark and Mateo unblend, listen, and speak differently. As they slowed down, listened inside, and listened to each other about what their parts found most threatening, their vigilant, wary protectors unblended further. But since listening can be scary for protective parts, Mark and Mateo's protectors sometimes popped back in. In anticipation of this, the therapist had asked Mark (the listening partner) if he was getting a "genuine yes," a yes with no caveats from other parts inside. This inquiry helps the listening person scan carefully for objections. Taking the time to connect with the listener's concerned parts helps them relax back. As Mateo and Mark experienced talking without becoming dysregulated, they were able to be as honest and vulnerable as they had hoped.

Therapist Handout

HELPING COUPLES BEGIN HARD CONVERSATIONS

This handout, which details more U-turn questions, illustrates how therapists can help partners unblend, speak for their parts, and listen from the Self. These queries can teach couples how to have any kind of difficult conversation without self-attack or hurting their partner. If a particular conversation causes trepidation in advance, start by talking about having the conversation.

First Inquiry

- Check inside: "When you think about having this hard conversation, what comes up? Which parts activate? What are their concerns?"

- "Instead of speaking *from* your parts (e.g., *I'm anxious about looking into my anger*), speak *for* your parts (*I have a part who feels anxious about finding out why I get so angry*)."

Second Inquiry

- Check inside: "What is the cost of *not* speaking up and *not* having this conversation successfully? Again, speak *for* your parts."

Third Inquiry

- Check inside: "How do your parts impact your partner? Speak *for* your parts as you consider their impact."

Fourth Inquiry

- Check inside: "What is your intention in having this conversation? What outcome do you want for you, for your partner, and for your relationship? Speak *for* your parts about their intentions."

Copyright © 2021, Toni Herbine-Blank, Martha Sweezy, *Internal Family Systems Couple Therapy Skills Manual*. All rights reserved.

COURAGEOUS COMMUNICATION TOOLBOX: TIPS FOR CLIENTS

- Unblending from your protectors is the key to successful communication. To unblend, experiment with doing a U-turn. How much of this reactivity is your own material? How much is about your partner?

- Make a date to practice speaking and listening well.

- Try speaking vulnerably *for* your parts.

- Experiment with softening your protectors so you can listen.

- Try acknowledging your partner's feelings and experiences before presenting your own.

- Revise blaming language, and practice speaking for your own feelings and needs.

- If you feel overwhelmed, *pause* and come back to the conversation in 20 minutes.

- When you make requests, pay attention to timing. Is this a good moment to bring up this topic?

- Practice making sense of your partner's experience, even if you don't feel like it.

- Reward small attempts at better communication with gratitude and appreciation.

Addressing Emotional Needs with Courageous Communication

Human beings have a biological need to attach, bond, love, and feel secure in their intimate relationships. Babies, as we know, thrive on securely connected interactions (Siegel, 2003). Similarly, intimate relationships thrive when emotional needs are met. However, when clients acknowledge their emotional needs and make requests but are shamed in response, a sense of inadequacy and anger are likely outcomes. In the context of IFIO therapy, these feelings are a window into the client's confusion about what they need and how to make clear requests.

There are a variety of reasons why people struggle to understand their own needs. Many were shamed for having needs early in life. The IFIO approach stipulates that taking care of one's own emotional needs is as essential as caring for a partner. This viewpoint is not intended to make people become islands of self-dependency but to foster self-love. At the same time, when each partner gives *and* receives love freely, understanding their partner's vulnerabilities, the result is deeper mutuality and secure attachment.

To help couples communicate courageously about emotional needs, therapists can follow these six steps:

1. Listen for and name the unmet needs below the client's anger.
2. Help partners identify their pattern of protection (e.g., fight, flee, shut down).
3. Help partners validate and unblend from frustrated protectors who attempt to get needs met in harmful ways.
4. Support each partner in doing a U-turn to explore hidden meanings and core emotional needs.
5. Assist the couple in doing a re-turn so they can request—not demand—that an emotional need be met.
6. Help each partner experiment with *giving* and *receiving* in the moment.

COMMUNICATING WITH COURAGE

The following case vignette illustrates how the U-turn reveals underlying emotional needs. Ulma and Cooper, a cisgendered, European-American, heterosexual couple in their early thirties, came to therapy for help communicating. They loved each other but had volatile and discouraging fights in which their protectors blamed one another and got angry in the hope of changing the other person. After a fight, they would move away from each other to try to regulate themselves, but they rarely returned to the conversation to reconnect positively. Their sessions often began with finger-pointing. In this session, Cooper launched the attack.

Cooper: What the hell, Ulma! How many times do I have to say that texting and texting when you feel insecure is not the way to get my attention? How many times a day?

Ulma: Way to freakin' embarrass me, Cooper! You make me sound like a total idiot.

Cooper: You act like an idiot. What can I say?

Therapist: Okay, let's hold on and back up. Cooper, it sounds like you're frustrated and need something from Ulma. Am I right?

Cooper: Frustrated yes, need something yes! I need her to change this behavior. It's nuts.

Therapist: [*to Ulma*] This communication from Cooper right now. How is it landing?

Ulma: It's humiliating.

Therapist: That makes sense to me. Can you hold on for a minute while I get curious with Cooper about this part?

Ulma: Please, whatever you have to do. I do not like being portrayed in this way.

Therapist: Cooper, I wonder if we could pause here and notice your frustration. Where is it in or around your body?

> *Inviting a U-turn by asking the client to notice himself and his body*

Cooper: In my chest and arms.

> *Locating the part in the body*

Therapist: Where is it most intense?

> *Anchoring the part in the body by inviting the client to be very specific*

Cooper: My chest.

Therapist: Do you recognize this sensation?

Cooper: I do.

Therapist: Does it have any information for you?

Cooper: It's a fight-or-flight thing.

> *Naming the ANS response*

Therapist: What is your strongest impulse?

Cooper: I want to fight. I want Ulma to hear me!

Therapist: Can you recognize this impulse as a part of you but not all of you?

> *Checking for unblending*

Cooper: Yes.

Therapist: Then let's say hi to this part. And notice how you feel toward it.

> *Befriending the part*

Cooper: [*sighs and focuses inward*] I feel okay. I know this feeling.

Therapist: What do you know about it?

Cooper: It means I'm afraid.

Therapist: A part of you is afraid?

> *Asserting the importance of parts language*

Cooper: Maybe that I can't meet all of her needs?

Therapist: And what else does the part say?

Cooper: I'll never get what I need.

Therapist: Which is?

Cooper: I don't even know…

Therapist: This is important. So let's be sure we understand. You have needs. But what are they? Your needs can't get through to you. And then Ulma comes along and seems to be expecting you to do something about her needs. I'm guessing this all feels like too much for your frustrated part. Who will meet all of these needs, inside and out?

> *Naming the projection: "When your protectors exile your needs, they will also exile her needs."*

Cooper: Yeah. Who will?

At this point, the therapist invited Cooper to speak *for* his frustrated part. We always aim for unblended speech, which fosters a *re-turn* to the partner with a broader perspective, a relaxed nervous system, and the readiness to reconnect. When we speak for a part, we honor its need to be heard clearly, which helps it be willing to unblend.

Therapist: That is a great question, Cooper. Let me help. Okay? First, I'll invite you to experiment with speaking *for* your frustrated part with Ulma.

Cooper: You mean instead of always saying what the part is upset about?

Therapist: That's right. I want you to speak to Ulma about what you just learned inside, starting with what happened in your body and moving to the fears.

Cooper: [*turning to Ulma*] You heard all that, right?

Ulma: I did. I'm grateful to hear it like that instead of the usual way. And I wouldn't mind hearing it again. Less choppy.

Cooper: Okay. First, I notice that when you ask for attention—especially in the middle of the day—I get physically agitated, and then I start a fight with you. I know this doesn't go well. I have fears. One, that I can't meet your needs, and two, I keep hearing, "What about me? What about my needs? Is she paying attention to what it might be like for me right now?" I don't know how to be successful in this area, so a part of me gets frustrated and pushes back. When I experience myself as incompetent or not taken into consideration, it's not my strong suit. I can't handle that.

In contrast to Cooper's opening statement ("What the hell, Ulma!"), Cooper and Ulma were now able to communicate more vulnerably, addressing their fears and needs.

Ulma: I hear you and that makes sense. It would be great to know what you need. I have no idea.

Cooper: That makes two of us.

Therapist: How was this communication compared to the way you usually speak and listen?

Ulma: So much better! Thank you.

Therapist: Cooper?

Cooper: Better, I guess. But now I just feel... empty and sad.

Therapist: I'm not surprised. I know this is painful. We will help that part too. Our next step will be discovering what you need and inviting Ulma to meet those needs.

> *Offering possibility*

❧

This vignette illustrates the IFIO therapist proffering a non-threatening invitation to one partner to do a U-turn, explore their feelings safely, unblend from activated parts, speak for their fears, and then re-turn to relational connection. The following **U-Turn and Re-Turn for Couples** worksheet provides a simple seven-step exercise that clients can use to help reactive parts unblend so they can speak to each other with insight rather than fear. This exercise can also be useful between sessions.

In addition, the **A Choice in Every Moment** worksheet helps couples break their patterns of reaction and counterreaction as they try to get their emotional needs met. Couples in conflict are generally blended with protective parts who believe that the only way to get their needs met is to counter the other person. This worksheet illustrates how partners can respond more effectively once they understand the following: (1) a knee-jerk response signals an unmet need; (2) by tracking under their frustration, they will discover the needs of a part who is stuck in a toxic childhood event; and (3) requests imbued with Self-energy are far more persuasive than demands from edgy protectors.

Finally, the **Finding and Speaking from Emotional Needs** worksheet can help clients slow down, make a U-turn, and explore deep longings and needs that were exiled in childhood, which are not being met in their current relationship. After using the worksheet to write about what they learned, invite clients to re-turn and speak from an unblended place for their parts, and then have them experiment with making requests.

In IFIO, we believe that the ability to ask and respond to emotional needs is key to intimacy. Since it's best for clients to practice making requests in session before doing so at home, we suggest helping them complete the exercise in session.

Client Worksheet

THE U-TURN AND RE-TURN FOR COUPLES

Learning to make a U-turn, unblend from reactive parts, and speak *for* them instead of *from* them is the key to having hard conversations safely. The process supports each person in gaining clarity, calming the nervous system, and getting perspective on the needs beneath their reactivity. This worksheet is a roadmap for the U-turn and can be used in the office with the help of a therapist or in between sessions.

1. Pause, breathe, and do a U-turn by focusing your attention inward.

2. Pay attention to your body. Describe your:

    Breathing

    _____

    Heart rate

    _____

    Muscle tension

    _____

    Inner voices

    _____

    Impulses

    _____

3. Befriend the parts you notice by saying hi and letting them know you're here to listen and learn. What do you say to these parts?

    _____

    _____

4. Explore your part's fears and vulnerabilities.

    What do they fear?

    _____

    _____

Copyright © 2021, Toni Herbine-Blank, Martha Sweezy, *Internal Family Systems Couple Therapy Skills Manual*. All rights reserved.

What's under that fear?

_____

_____

What do they need?

_____

_____

5. Report what you learned.

    In my body, I noticed:

    _____

    _____

    I have a part who fears:

    _____

    _____

6. Speak for these parts.

    I have a part who needs:

    _____

    _____

    I have a part who wants:

    _____

    _____

7. Make a request from the Self. What is the core need?

    _____

    _____

Copyright © 2021, Toni Herbine-Blank, Martha Sweezy, *Internal Family Systems Couple Therapy Skills Manual.* All rights reserved.

Client Worksheet

A CHOICE IN EVERY MOMENT

In relationships, we often view frustration and anger as protective attempts to get emotional needs met. With the help of your therapist, use this worksheet to understand the emotional needs behind your frustration or anger and to learn to make requests from your Self instead of making demands from protectors. Partners respond better to an invitation than an obligation.

1. Focusing on your feeling of frustration, what do you notice?

   _____

   _____

2. What words do you hear?

   _____

   _____

3. What is your normal ("knee-jerk") response when you are frustrated?

   _____

   _____

4. Which parts of you react (e.g., controlling, angry, impatient, manipulative, submissive, analyzing)?

   _____

   _____

5. What response does your reaction elicit from your partner's parts?

   _____

   _____

6. What happens *inside* you when you get this response from your partner's parts (e.g., angry, sad, happy, excited, anxious)?

   _____

   _____

Copyright © 2021, Toni Herbine-Blank, Martha Sweezy, *Internal Family Systems Couple Therapy Skills Manual*. All rights reserved.

7. What do you notice about this cycle of reaction and counterreaction between your protective parts and your partner's protective parts?

_____

_____

8. Can you see, feel, or sense the vulnerable part underneath your protector's frustrated reaction? What do you know about that part?

_____

_____

9. What pattern of interactions or incidents in childhood wounded you?

_____

_____

10. What core need did your young, wounded part look for but not get (e.g., to be heard, noticed, loved, witnessed, held, understood, feel connected)?

_____

_____

Copyright © 2021, Toni Herbine-Blank, Martha Sweezy, *Internal Family Systems Couple Therapy Skills Manual*. All rights reserved.

Client Worksheet

FINDING AND SPEAKING FOR EMOTIONAL NEEDS

This exercise is a clarifier. Feelings (and the needs they speak for) find expression in the body before becoming conscious thought. By turning to the body with our full attention, we tap into a wealth of crucial information. As the poet, Rumi, said, "The cure for pain is in the pain. These pains you feel are messengers. Listen to them." After listening, speak for the parts you hear. When we listen to parts carefully and speak for their needs, we receive their gifts in return.

1. Close your eyes, take a few deep breaths, and turn your focus inward. Think of a person in your life with whom you have an intimate connection who can anger or frustrate you. Call that person up in your mind's eye and invite them to do or say that angering or frustrating thing. Observe your reactions:

    What do you feel in your body?

    _____

    _____

    What do you hear yourself saying to yourself?

    _____

    _____

    What feelings are you aware of?

    _____

    _____

    What is your first impulse?

    _____

    _____

    Can you recognize this impulse as a "part" of you?

    _____

    _____

Copyright © 2021, Toni Herbine-Blank, Martha Sweezy, *Internal Family Systems Couple Therapy Skills Manual*. All rights reserved.

2. Now let the image of this person float away, and invite your reactive part to turn toward you and begin a gentle inquiry:

What is your role?

_____

_____

What are you concerned would happen if you didn't react this way?

_____

_____

Who are you protecting?

_____

_____

What vulnerability concerns you?

_____

_____

What childhood incident(s) launched this pattern of reactivity?

_____

_____

3. Now ask yourself: What did this young part of you need and not get from an adult at that time? Listen for core needs, like the need to be heard, noticed, loved, witnessed, held, understood, or to know you are not alone. Relax and listen. Don't push for an answer or rush your parts. Allow them to take their time and give you information.

_____

_____

4. Are you available to meet those needs internally right now? Can you be present to that child in the here and now? Why or why not?

_____

_____

Copyright © 2021, Toni Herbine-Blank, Martha Sweezy, *Internal Family Systems Couple Therapy Skills Manual*. All rights reserved.

5. To end this inquiry, thank your parts for any and all information, no matter how much or how little. And then check in again with your reactive part. How is it feeling?

_____

_____

6. Finally, ponder this question: What would it be like to speak for those underlying needs instead of speaking from your reactive parts?

_____

_____

Copyright © 2021, Toni Herbine-Blank, Martha Sweezy, *Internal Family Systems Couple Therapy Skills Manual*. All rights reserved.

Giving and Receiving with Courageous Communication

Giving and receiving love, care, and support in intimate relationships is a complex process for several reasons. Partners in a reciprocal relationship generally establish either an overt or a covert contract that governs how and when their needs will or will not be met. When these agreements are covert, partners struggle that much more to identify what feels loving and to express love in ways their partner will be able to receive.

Because systems need balance, imbalance in a relationship erodes the confidence and security of partners, especially when the imbalance continues over time. For example, let's say the strong caretaking parts of one partner activate the longing for rescue in their partner's exiles. The longing of exiles, in turn, rouses vigilant, reactive protectors whose mission is to protect those exiles. These parts view the caretaking behavior as potentially disappointing and oppressive. They are scared of the caretaker—not grateful. When they lash out, the caretaker is surprised and hurt, and believes their partner is ungrateful. In IFIO therapy, we want the couple to understand this kind of struggle over giving and receiving care.

GIVING AND RECEIVING

Reed and Sloane, a cisgendered, heterosexual, European-American couple in their early fifties, were both divorced and had only been together for a couple of years when they came to therapy with a goal of breaking old patterns that were endangering their relationship. Reed was a man of his community with a reputation for generosity and service to others. Sloane, an artist, had good friends but was more of an introvert. Sloane had recently been diagnosed with chronic fatigue syndrome and had less energy and stamina for a shared social life. They had been in therapy for more than a year when they had this discussion about giving and receiving.

Sloane: I want to say something. It's the time of year when people give parties, and we've been invited to two over the coming weekend. We're going away next week, and just getting ready is a huge stretch for me—I'm not saying it should be, just that it is. So I told Reed I can't go to the parties. But I have a part who thinks I'm a drag and worries about losing him. So [*turning to Reed*] I want you to know that I will go if you tell me that it's important to you. I'll go to either party or both.

Reed: Oh no. Why would you do that?

Sloane: For you. [*Reed looks down and fidgets*]

   Therapist: Can I jump in here? [*they nod*] What are you feeling right now, Reed?

Reed: My skin is crawling.

   Therapist: What are you hearing?

Reed: "We don't do that!"

   Therapist: Who is that?

Reed: My father.

   Therapist: A part who sounds like your father or your father?

Reed: I don't know.

Therapist: Ask.

Reed: A part.

Therapist: And why is it representing your father right now?

Reed: "Father knows best!" [*everyone laughs*]

Therapist: And what does this father part have to say about giving and receiving?

Reed: "Don't be selfish!"

Therapist: What would be selfish?

Reed: Needs.

Therapist: So let's do a thought experiment. How would it feel if you were to say to Sloane right now, "Yes please do come! It means a lot to me to have you by my side at the party. I want you there."

Reed: [*wrinkling his nose*] I can't do that!

Sloane: You can't?

Therapist: Let me slow you down here. You, Reed, have a part who is allergic to receiving. And you, Sloane, have a part who feels something about that response. What do you feel?

Sloane: Diminished.

Therapist: [*to Reed*] Do you understand that?

Reed: We must be onto something because I have a part who is yelling, "No! No! No! No!"

Therapist: Can we check in with that part? [*Reed nods, the therapist looks at Sloane*]

Sloane: Go for it.

Therapist: How do you feel toward the part who just said no?

Reed: Sorry for it.

Therapist: What is it concerned about?

Reed: Weakness.

Therapist: Receiving is weak?

Reed: I guess so.

Therapist: [*to Sloane*] Does Reed do things for you?

Sloane: He's the soul of generosity.

   Therapist: How do you make sense of Sloane's annoyance when you're so generous?

Reed: [*chuckling*] Do I have to?

   Therapist: Can I guess? I want your parts to tell me what I get wrong.

Reed: Please.

   Therapist: You have a part we know pretty well who wants you to be good so you'll be loved. He protects a little boy whose father could terrify him, and he couldn't go complaining to his mother. Right so far? [*Reed nods*] And you have another part, a rebellious teenager, who doesn't want to be good. Sometimes he just takes over and acts rude and selfish. Right? [*Reed and Sloane nod*] And people are shocked by that teenage part.

Sloane: That would be me!

   Therapist: The teenager desperately wants to be free and unconstrained by the good boy.

Reed: Yes.

   Therapist: So who wants you to do all this giving: the good boy or the rebel?

Reed: The good boy, without a doubt.

   Therapist: How do you feel toward him now?

Reed: [*shaking his head*] I'm amazed he's still going so strong.

   Therapist: And given how strong he is, how do you feel toward him?

Reed: I wish he'd go away. [*before the therapist can respond, Sloane speaks*]

Sloane: [*nods*] The teenager hurts me and makes me mad sometimes, but the good boy scares me.

   Therapist: [*to Reed*] Are you open to hearing about that?

Reed: Yes.

Sloane: If receiving is weak—and you do help me, and I do receive your help—then what am I? [*Reed nods thoughtfully*] How can I accept your help if I can't do anything for you in return? When you refuse my help, I feel small and… insignificant.

Reed: I hear you. But I just can't imagine changing.

   Therapist: What's the fear?

Reed: I'll be bad.

   Therapist: And then?

Reed: [*after a long pause*] I'll feel small and insignificant.

   Therapist: The boy?

Reed: It always comes back to him. Why hasn't he been helped yet?

   Therapist: Yeah, why?

Reed: Fear?

   Therapist: Of him?

Reed: Of being like him.

   Therapist: What is he like?

Reed: Insignificant and weak!

   Therapist: Can we get permission to help him?

Reed: [*shakes his head in amazement*] I don't think so. I'm not getting a yes on that.

Sloane: Who won't let you help him?

Reed: Well… there's a part who says, "What about me?"

   Therapist: Is that the good boy speaking? [*Reed nods*] How do you feel toward him right now?

Reed: I care about him.

   Therapist: If we help the little one, wouldn't that help the good boy too?

Reed: But what would happen to me?

> *Speaking from the good boy part*

   Therapist: [*speaking to the good boy part directly*] You won't disappear. There's room for everyone. [*Reed is silent*] Can we do a little experiment? [*they nod*] Okay. Reed ask Sloane to move closer to you. [*Reed looks paralyzed.*]

   Therapist: What's happening to you right now?

Reed: It's hard.

   Therapist: What are you hearing?

Reed: "We don't ask others to do our dirty work."

   Therapist: If you were to ask Sloane to sit closer to you right now, what need would you be asking her to fill?

Reed: To feel less alone. [*looking at Sloane*] To know I was a priority. To know I don't always have to worry about other people. To feel important. [*Sloane slides across the couch and takes one of Reed's hands. He blinks tears away. They are silent.*] I can barely breathe.

Therapist: What would happen if you breathed?

Reed: [*Covers his eyes, leans forward and weeps. When his breath calms, he sits up and looks from Sloane to the therapist and back.*] I would grieve.

❧

Balanced give-and-take in a partnership is essential. As we see in this couple's interaction, the burden of equating giving with strength and receiving with weakness undermines the balance in their intimacy. Of course, the person who refuses to receive discourages others from giving, but that is only part of this burden's cost. Ultimately, one person not receiving either sours the other person on receiving or puts them in the position of a child. Reed's good boy part feared losing his job and his reason for existing, but when Reed spoke for his underlying needs, the good boy's opposition melted for the moment, and Reed was able to feel sad. Just as internal shifts flow outward, relational shifts flow inward.

Projection: The Cost of Hidden Parts

Our protectors respond to attachment injury by hiding those parts of us who seem vulnerable, who seem to create the conditions for more injury. In order to disown the dangerous vulnerability of these exiled parts, clients often engage in projection by criticizing a disowned quality as it shows up (or seems to show up) in others. Managers who project criticize internally and then externally. For example, if a client's family (or culture) frowns on direct expressions of anger, their managers will make a big effort to suppress and hide parts who get angry. Projection is one way of doing this. We see this when one partner's angry protector insists that the other person in the couple is the angry one: *I'm not angry, you're angry.* When we project, we reject not only our own important feelings (and parts), but also the actual feelings (and parts) of the other person.

When a couple's interpersonal conflicts center on projection, we can use the following two U-turn exercises to help them take back their projections and love their disowned parts.

The first of these U-turn exercises illustrates how protectors project vulnerability and place blame for suffering on others. When this exercise is done with respect, it can help partners befriend some of their most difficult or elusive parts. The second U-turn exercise presented here helps partners notice the ways in which they abandon their injured parts when they let their protectors jump to the barricades. While the U-turn is tremendously beneficial in any relational conflict, it can be a challenge.

Clients may feel disoriented as they bring the qualities their protectors have tried to hide with projection (insisting they are features of someone else) to light. Therefore, we start by helping clients honor these protectors and understand their motives.

Client Worksheet

DO A U-TURN WITH YOUR PARTS

"Doing a U-turn" means turning your attention inside, to your own parts, when you have a feeling or reaction to someone else that you want to learn more about. Most of us have protectors who deflect attention from vulnerability by downplaying the importance and meaning of our feelings (that is, the feelings of other parts internally) by insisting that some external person caused us to feel that way. Instead of taking this inner voice of blame at face value, we can treat it as a signal that some other part of us, either another protector or an exile, needs to be heard. The U-turn liberates us from the paralysis and powerlessness of blame.

1. First, think of someone in your life who offends you. Make this personal. What does this person do or say that is offensive? Listen to your judging part as you describe them.

   _____

   _____

2. Then ask yourself the following questions:

   What do your parts want this person to *do* differently?

   _____

   _____

   Who do your parts want this person to *be* for you?

   _____

   _____

   What advice do your parts have for this person?

   _____

   _____

   Let your critic judge this person without censoring. List your thoughts about the person's behavior in this situation.

   _____

   _____

Copyright © 2021, Toni Herbine-Blank, Martha Sweezy, *Internal Family Systems Couple Therapy Skills Manual*. All rights reserved.

What is it about this situation that your parts don't ever want you to experience again?

_____

_____

In order to feel less offended and be happier in a relationship with this person, how do your parts want you to act with this person?

_____

_____

3. Now ask the critic to give you some space inside to be curious and to listen, and when you can feel that space, do a U-turn. First, turn global criticisms about this person into factual observations.

_____

_____

4. Now ask yourself: When someone treats me badly, how do I treat myself? Do my parts criticize me? Do my parts plot revenge? Do my parts repeatedly avoid accepting and feeling sad about what happened by rehearsing a different scenario with a different outcome? If so, ask them: Whom do you protect?

_____

_____

5. Once you have uncovered the part of you who is being protected, with permission, ask that part: What happens to you while these other parts are criticizing, plotting, and undoing?

_____

_____

6. Now check again: Do you still have space inside to be curious and to listen? If so, inquire about which of your parts are involved in the relationship with this person, and consider how your parts behave. Make a list of these parts, and set an intention to get to know them better.

_____

_____

Adapted from the work of Byron Katie

Copyright © 2021, Toni Herbine-Blank, Martha Sweezy, *Internal Family Systems Couple Therapy Skills Manual*. All rights reserved.

Client Worksheet

A U-TURN IN A THOUGHT EXPERIMENT

It's not easy to notice our own projections—protectors who use this strategy don't intend us to notice ourselves at all. This thought experiment asks you to revisit an activating situation by going inside and noticing in hindsight. This is a good way to introduce yourself to protective parts who only come out for emergencies and can otherwise be hard to find. This is an opportunity to meet your protectors and find your exiles.

1. Go back to a situation when someone hurt you. Notice how your protectors reacted. Did they immediately start thinking about what to *do*? If so, what was it? And what did they do? Did your response include: insisting on being understood correctly, complying to forestall conflict, or plotting for revenge? Jot down whatever you learn.

   _____

   _____

2. Now ask the parts who reacted to join you in answering these questions:

   Which part got hurt in that situation?

   _____

   _____

   What happened to the hurt part when other parts reacted?

   _____

   _____

   Will the reactive parts give you permission to help the part who got hurt? Why or why not?

   _____

   _____

   Would the hurt part like help? Why or why not?

   _____

   _____

Copyright © 2021, Toni Herbine-Blank, Martha Sweezy, *Internal Family Systems Couple Therapy Skills Manual*. All rights reserved.

3. Then consider these questions:

Have I behaved in the same (hurtful) way with other people? How so?

_____

_____

Do I have parts who act this way internally? If so, which parts?

_____

_____

What other parts of this person have I noticed?

_____

_____

How do those parts behave? Make a list.

_____

_____

Copyright © 2021, Toni Herbine-Blank, Martha Sweezy, *Internal Family Systems Couple Therapy Skills Manual*. All rights reserved.

Intrapsychic Work in Couple Therapy: Going Inside

At various points in IFIO couple therapy, one partner bears witness as the other explores their inner experience. We typically do this individual work within couple therapy for one of these reasons: (1) one partner has a part who is highly charged and won't unblend, (2) patterns of behavior appear entrenched, or (3) negative childhood experiences or shame about having needs begin to surface. While unconventional, individual work in the context of couple therapy can be deeply healing. When a person attends to their wounded, burdened parts with compassion, they re-turn to their partner feeling safer, calmer, braver, and, thus, more available. The inner security that comes from accessing the Self sets the table for acknowledging how negative beliefs (e.g., "I'm unlovable") have impacted their relationship and their partner.

Meanwhile, the witnessing partner sees that vulnerability while also seeing their loved one's strength, resilience, and presence. In many cases, this shared experience challenges the couple's view of each other as just the "wounder" or the "caretaker," and gives them freedom to explore what they actually need and want in their relationship today. When intimate relationships become challenging, implicit memories based on preverbal experiences will begin to surface. We aim to bring implicit memories into awareness so that, over time, the couple can change their perceptions, feelings, and thoughts about themselves and each other (Badenoch, 2008).

In addition to showing partners how childhood experiences influence adult behavior, there are other benefits to individual work in the context of couple therapy. First, the partner who is engaging in self-exploration promotes secure attachments between the Self and their parts, helping parts heal from negative beliefs acquired during childhood. Second, the witnessing partner takes an active role in their partner's healing process by listening with empathy and compassion to painful childhood dilemmas. When one person is inside witnessing a wounded, vulnerable part with deep love and caring, and their partner holds that vulnerability with love and caring as well, a positive cycle of healing ensues. The inclusive nature of the IFIO model invites relational healing inside and out.

GOING INSIDE

Step One: Contract with the couple and let them know that one person will be going inside while the other serves as a witness.

Step Two: Support the witnessing person to unblend so they can listen and stay present. Remind them that you are there to help if they become afraid or reactive.

Step Three: Gently and respectfully encourage unblending, and help the client establish a compassionate connection with themselves internally. Pay close attention to protectors in both partners to maintain a safe working environment, and continually check for ANS activation.

Step Four: Unburden exiles if appropriate and time allows.

Step Five: Foster and support interpersonal connection and co-regulation.

GOING INSIDE

Mark and Mateo, the couple we introduced earlier who were seeking therapy to improve communication challenges surrounding sex, were doing well with practicing safe, respectful communications, as well as speaking for protective parts and scared young exiles. They had learned to wait before trying to solve problems. They had learned the value of speaking and listening skillfully, which strengthened their understanding of themselves and each other and led to more closeness. However, a small voice inside Mateo continued to ask for help, which warranted additional inner exploration. The following dialogue illustrates how the therapist helped him attend to that part.

Therapist: At the end of the last session, Mateo, we decided to listen to the voice who speaks of being broken and damaged. Do you remember?

Mateo: I do, and I took your advice and didn't minimize it when I noticed it this week. That was challenging, though, because I find it embarrassing.

Therapist: Say more.

Mateo: Thinking about it and then trying to speak about it seems weak. *So* vulnerable. I have this strong feeling that I'd rather not.

Therapist: You have parts who judge this voice and push it away?

Mark: [*chiming in*] Yes, he does! Even I notice how much he dislikes this part. Not that I don't get it.

Mateo: Listening to my negative headspace… It's just not something I did before having cancer.

Therapist: How do you feel about listening for a little bit now? Let's ask all parts who judge this voice if they're willing to let you listen.

Mateo: I don't feel much resistance at the moment. Let's try. [*closes his eyes*]

Therapist: I'm just going to check in with Mark. [*to Mark*] Are you available? Heart open? [*he nods*] If for any reason either of you starts to feel uncomfortable, activated, sleepy, or just unable to stay present, please let me know.

> Helping Mark's parts unblend

Mark: I will.

Mateo: Okay.

Therapist: Ready, Mateo?

Mateo: I was just remembering how important it felt to be invincible when I was a boy. I got beat up a few times. And coming out in high school was a nightmare. So I made it a mission to be strong, healthy, desirable, and unstoppable.

Therapist: Could we name that as a part of you?

Mateo: Yes! A great part of me.

Therapist: And who does that part protect?

Mateo: I see where you're going. The weak, vulnerable boy who got bullied.

> *Naming the exile*

Therapist: That's right. Can you see him in your mind's eye?

Mateo: [*leaning back, eyes closed*] Yes.

Therapist: How do you feel toward him?

> *Checking for unblending*

Mateo: I feel sorry for him.

Therapist: Is that pity or concern?

> *Checking again for unblending*

Mateo: Not pity. Kind, open. He's small, which makes him a big target.

Therapist: For whom?

Mateo: His brothers and other kids.

Therapist: Is he aware of you?

> *Fostering the Self-to-part connection*

Mateo: Yes.

Therapist: Are you available to listen to him?

Mateo: I am.

Therapist: Let him know.

> *Developing the relationship*

Therapist: [*connecting with Mark*] Are you able to listen? [*Mark nods*]

Mateo: Being bullied sucks.

Therapist: Can he tell you or show you?

Mateo: [*nods*] He's showing me.

> *Witnessing*

Therapist: Is that okay?

Mateo: It's a flood. I feel overwhelmed.

Therapist: What does he need from you so he can dial the intensity back?

Mateo: He's afraid I won't stay with him. He thinks if he slows down, I'll push him away.

Therapist: Other parts would like to push him away? Have pushed him away before?

> Naming protectors who feel threatened by the exile

Mateo: It's true.

Therapist: What do you say to him?

Mateo: [*voice soft*] I'm listening. I'm right here.

Therapist: How does he respond?

Mateo: The images are slowing down.

Therapist: Can you stay with him?

Mateo: Yes. [*the therapist looks over to Mark, who gives a thumbs up*]

> Checking in with the witnessing partner periodically to maintain connection

Therapist: What are you noticing now, Mateo?

Mateo: So much sadness and anger. He's upset. Everyone seemed to need a scapegoat—someone to beat up, put down, hurt. Where was the help? He's asking why he wasn't protected.

Therapist: What do you say?

Mateo: [*shaking his head*] I'm so sorry.

Therapist: Is there a specific incident he needs to show you?

Mateo: He's showing me how his brothers stuffed him in the dryer at the laundromat. [*Mark grimaces*] He couldn't stop them. I remember the fear that they would turn it on and the nausea. They didn't, thank God. He threw up in the wastebasket when he got out and they teased him about that.

Therapist: What did he need from an adult then?

Mateo: To get him out of there and set his brothers straight.

Therapist: Can you do that for him?

Mateo: I can.

Therapist: What does he want you to say or do that he needed a grown-up to do then?

Mateo: [*nods*] He's telling me. I'm doing it. [*a few moments of silence*] I'm speaking to his brothers.

Therapist: What did he conclude about himself after that?

Mateo: He felt weak, broken, incapable, worthless.

Therapist: That's a lot for a young boy.

Mateo: This is so sad!

Therapist: How are you feeling toward him now?

Mateo: I see what happened. He didn't deserve any of that. I want to take care of him.

Therapist: Does he know?

Mateo: He does.

Therapist: Where are you both now?

Mateo: He's here with me in the present.

> *Spontaneous retrieval from the past to the present*

Therapist: Would he like to unload those beliefs?

> *Inviting the exile to unburden, if he's ready*

Mateo: I think that's all we can do for today. I think I just need to be with him.

> *Not ready to unburden yet*

Therapist: Sounds good. Will he stay with you?

> *Honoring the request to stop*

Mateo: He's with me. [*looks at Mark*]

Therapist: Can he see Mark?

Mateo: Yes. He sees that Mark's heart is open. That helps.

Mark: Wow, Mateo! I've heard stories about your brothers. I know them now, of course. But you've never mentioned the dryer. Unbelievable! I'm so sorry.

Mateo: No wonder I needed to be strong.

> *Connecting the past to the present*

Therapist: And we'll come back to that.

We only do individual work in a couple session if we expect the witnessing partner is capable of being truly available. The witnessing partner helps the other regulate and stay Self-led. The therapist stays connected with both partners and checks in with the witnessing part periodically, either by eye contact or with words. When the client's Self and the witnessing partner extend compassion to the exile together, the result is a *relational unburdening*. Although relational healing is powerful, the timing must be right. On the other hand, sometimes we want to see the partners individually. We suggest individual work for partners when:

1. Couple therapy isn't safe due to emotional or physical violence.
2. The couple asks that each partner have time with you alone.
3. One or both partners prefer to be seen separately to discuss sex or sexuality.

Some therapists routinely meet with a couple once and then see each partner individually for a session before bringing them back together. Some never do this. Yet others decide on a case-by-case basis. In IFIO, we have no particular recommendation. Our primary focus is on the couple and their relationship. We maintain this focus when we see partners alone, whether once or for several sessions. Every practitioner must assess the situation at hand and make this decision on their own. However, if you do decide to see partners individually, you'll want to avoid these common pitfalls:

1. Forgetting to address how individual sessions fit their contract for the therapy.
2. Neglecting to clarify your policy on secrets.
3. Failing to clarify that individual sessions will focus on supporting the relationship and that you are a therapist for their relationship.
4. Causing an imbalance in the therapeutic alliance by seeing one person and not the other.
5. Causing an imbalance in the therapeutic alliance by making one partner the identified patient and agreeing to see this partner individually.

Talking with the couple ahead of time about the reasons for having an individual session and establishing guidelines regarding secrets creates safety. For example, some therapists keep strict boundaries by telling clients they will not keep secrets. Others invite secrets with the understanding that they will help the client reveal these secrets in the context of the therapy. Others feel comfortable holding a secret. We encourage all IFIO therapists to listen to their parts on this issue and maintain integrity.

Shame as Shaming and Shamefulness

People shame each other both inadvertently and purposefully in relationships. In IFIO, we view external shaming as a well-disguised attempt to distract from inner shaming and feelings of shamefulness. Therapists can orient to the active, viral nature of shame by doing three things:

• First, by talking with clients about parts.
• Second, by speaking and writing about shame as an action (shaming) or a state of being (shameful). Viewing shame this way steers us to attend to the internal relational drama that stems from attachment injuries in childhood. In particular, children who feel unlovable or worthless in response to being shamed develop protective parts who feel compelled to take action. Ironically, proactive protectors tend to do a lot shaming inside while reactive protectors rebel by doing the opposite and behaving shamelessly or bullying others.
• Third, by befriending protectors who shame, inside or out. Our goal is to unburden exiles and free these protectors.

SHAMING AND SHAMEFULNESS

The following dialogue illustrates how these guidelines affected a session between one couple, Michaela and George. This cisgendered, heterosexual pair—one of whom (Michaela) was European American, the other of whom (George) had a Jamaican grandfather—came in to explore the issue of shame. Michaela mentioned feeling a lot of shame when her partner, George, would say things about her to other people, even positive things.

Michaela: I don't like being talked about. I feel exposed.

  Therapist: Were you aware of that, George?

George: Maybe a little. I didn't know it was a big deal.

Michaela: Truthfully, I haven't said much. I am always careful of his feelings. And then another part gets mad because I'm tiptoeing around.

George: Who says you have to tiptoe around?

  Therapist: Let me jump in here. [*to Michaela*] You have a part who is careful not to shame him?

Michaela: When he feels shamed, he gets mad. Like now. That's why I don't say anything.

George: I'm not mad! You're always telling me what I feel.

  Therapist: Can I interrupt? [*they nod*] This dynamic is important. I'm going to sum up what I just heard. You, Michaela, have a part who feels exposed if George talks about you, and a part warns you not to say anything to him because it fears he will feel shamed and get mad, is that right? [*she nods*] And then you have another part who thinks you're tiptoeing around his anger and gets mad at him. Is that right?

Michaela: And mad at me.

  Therapist: I see. And then what happens?

Michaela: I criticize him for something.

  Therapist: And when she criticizes you, George, what do you do?

George: I get mad.

  Therapist: You have a part who gets mad. What happens just before this part gets mad?

George: I feel like a bad little boy.

  Therapist: So you have a part who feels he's being told he's a bad little boy and a part who gets mad about that?

George: Yes.

  Therapist: And do you have any parts inside who tell you that you're bad?

George: Yes. I have a part who says Michaela is right.

Michaela: You do?

George: Yes. But I don't agree with it.

Therapist: So one part tells you that her critic is right and another part disagrees. If I can just keep going with this for a moment? [*they nod*] I'm hearing that you both have parts who do some shaming inside and some parts who feel ashamed. And you've also identified parts in each other who do some external shaming—of each other. Is that right? [*they nod*] Is this news to you?

Michaela: Well kind of. I never thought of it this way. [*with a chuckle*] That's a whole lot of shaming going on!

Therapist: Indeed.

At this point, the therapist had summed up the shame cycle and pointed out that it was active in both partners. Both Michaela and George seem relieved after the therapist's summation. When Michaela chuckled, George leaned back in his chair.

George: Any hope for us?

Therapist: Yes. All this shaming, shamefulness, and anger may seem complicated. But it's common, and we can help your parts. Would you be willing to do a little inner inquiry? [*they nod*] Go inside and ask your shaming parts this question: "If we could help the parts who have been hurt so their feelings of shamefulness didn't pop up all the time, would you still need to criticize?"

George: No.

Michaela: My part says no too. But it doesn't believe anyone can change the past.

Asking protectors this hypothetical question is very important. First, it asserts that we can resolve the underlying problem that motivates the part's behavior. Second, it invites the part to think about its own future: What would happen if it had no motive to do this job? Once a protector names its problem (e.g., an exile who feels shameful), and the therapist suggests that the exile can be helped to feel better, protective parts often object and insist it's not possible. Since protective parts have never been able to resolve the underlying problem of shamefulness—and never will be able to—we validate their concern. At the same time, we assert that we do actually have a way of helping the exile.

Therapist: Your critic doesn't have to believe in a good outcome. It just has to be willing to try something new. Is it?

Michaela: Tentatively.

Therapist: Fair enough. So let me ask this question of you, Michaela, and then I'll ask George. Which came first, the parts who do all this shaming inside and out, or the feeling of being shameful?

Steering them to consider the origins of the burden that keeps their inner shame cycle going

Michaela: [*after a few moments of thought*] My mother is cold in a way. A lot of the time when I was a kid, she was sweet and fun, and then she would freeze me out with this look of contempt, and I never knew why. I couldn't see it coming. She would get angry and just walk away.

George: Her mother is crazy.

Michaela: I hate to admit it, but the critical voice inside *is* my mother.

Therapist: And the one who feels shameful?

Michaela: Is a little girl. I see her.

Therapist: So after her mother shamed her, another part took on the job of criticizing her inside? [*Michaela nods*] What does the critic want for her?

Michaela: Sounds silly when I hear it, but it says it wants her to be safe.

Therapist: Is this strategy working?

Michaela: No.

As this vignette illustrates, relational injury in childhood sets the stage for the relational fears of adults' protectors. Illuminating this inner shaming cycle helps partners connect the dots backward to the roots of protectors' fears, which include not only the original experience of being shamed, but the internal shaming that followed. When parts unblend and the Self is available, partners notice and can take responsibility for their own fierce internal shaming. If their partner is also shaming them, they become less vulnerable to it and more Self-led in response. If their partner is not shaming them, they can notice and take responsibility for the ways in which their protectors project.

The goal in IFIO is to open the door for couples to be different from each other and to have conversations that might be difficult with clarity, confidence, and courage. When they realize they have sufficient inner resources, they take relational risks more freely. Therefore, IFIO prioritizes assessing and healing the toxic effects of having been shamed in the past. In addition, we maintain that therapists can make no better investment than becoming knowledgeable about—and unafraid of—their own shaming and shamed parts. Therapists must notice any of their own parts who feel overwhelmed or want to avoid the client's shaming protectors or shameful exiles. In session, therapists can help these parts unblend by promising to return later. When shaming and shamed parts no longer evoke shamefulness in us, we become helpful.

In order to heal shaming and shamefulness in couple therapy, we make a clear contract for taking an active role as the therapist, and we seek permission to be directive (e.g., "I am going to slow you down"). We also reiterate the couple's shame cycle many times during a single session and over time throughout treatment, making sure to validate each partner's needs at the same time. Once the couple's shame cycle has been identified, we help each partner's shaming, blaming protectors unblend by focusing on the body and asking how the client feels toward that sensation. Shamefulness in the body is visible through a client's posture, eye contact, and tone of voice. We validate protectors by appreciating their intention to keep the client safe and for their efforts to help—and, at the same time, we validate the needs of wounded exiles. When we reach childhood events that had lasting sequelae in the form of extreme feeling states and burdensome beliefs, we can then release the client's protectors, as well as their exiles, in the presence of their partner.

HEALING THE WOUNDS OF SHAMING

The following case illustrates how shame wounds can be healed with the support of a partner. Gwen and Wyatt, a cisgendered, European-American, heterosexual couple in their late forties, came to therapy after their twin boys left home for college. They reported having focused on raising their boys and working to sustain a good lifestyle over the last 18 years. In the process, however, they had lost a sense of emotional and physical intimacy, and their relationship often felt unpleasant to both. Gwen had a habit of trying to get Wyatt's attention by belittling and shaming him. His protectors responded by trying to "get things right," but when that failed to quell her, they would stonewall and withdraw. At this point, the couple avoided conflict and lapsed into disconnected conversations, which left them feeling dissatisfied and hopeless. In therapy, they wanted to break the impasse and reconnect.

To do so, they learned about their protective impulses (most notably avoidance) and their emotional needs for acceptance and love, including how conflict arose when they were afraid these needs would not be met. Hypothesizing that their reactivity was linked to early experiences of shaming, the therapist began—slowly and respectfully—to support them in deepening their inner work. As the following dialogue with Wyatt illustrates, not all shame cycles involve rage and blame. Of course, Gwen also needed to explore her angry and vulnerable parts, which the therapist did at another time.

Gwen: [*frustrated*] I'm so tired of the same old dynamic day after day. You just don't want to be with me.

Wyatt: What are you talking about? I'm always trying to be with you. I try to figure out what you need. But all I know is that you're angry.

Gwen: That's not the same as being together. That's like… vigilance. You watch and wait.

> **Therapist:** [*to Gwen*] So you have a frustrated part who hopes for more connection with Wyatt. Right?

Naming parts and needs right away

Gwen: That's right.

> **Therapist:** [*to Wyatt*] And you have parts who try to connect with Gwen but don't succeed and experience her as angry. Am I right?

Checking for agreement

Wyatt: Yes! She's always angry. I can't get it right no matter how hard I try.

> **Therapist:** You both recognize this pattern? Gwen has a part with a need for connection and a frustrated part who speaks for that need, while Wyatt has a part who tries and tries to connect but never feels successful. [*to Wyatt*] And then what?

Identifying a recognizable pattern of protection

Wyatt: I go in my cave.

Therapist: [*to Wyatt*] And as you go in your cave, Gwen gets frustrated. And as she expresses frustration, you back away more. And the cycle continues until what happens?

Wyatt: I give up and disappear entirely.

Therapist: What does Gwen do then?

> *Checking for awareness of impact*

Wyatt: She disappears too, and we both feel awful.

Gwen: [*nods in agreement*] Like, why bother trying?

Therapist: This is your pattern. Shall we look at what is happening under your frustration and hopelessness to understand why this pattern is hard to break?

> *Reassuring exiles that we will look beyond protectors*

Wyatt: Sure. [*Gwen nods*]

Therapist: Gwen, it sounds like your frustrated part is here right now. Correct?

Gwen: Actually, I want to start over. Speaking from my frustration doesn't work, right? Could I start over?

At this point, Gwen caught her protector being critical. She paused and requested an opportunity to speak *for* that part instead of *from* it. Recognizing that her protector was hurting Wyatt and choosing to try a different behavior was relationally reparative.

Therapist: [*to Wyatt*] Are you available for Gwen to try something different?

> *Seeking permission*

Wyatt: [*smiling*] Sure!

Gwen: Look, it's true, I have needs that aren't being met, and I am the first to admit I'm not very skilled at asking. But … this part of me wants you to know that your part who tries so hard to figure out what I want and need is not getting it right. I don't need caretaking. And when I feel frustrated about that, you run away and I'm completely alone.

Therapist: [*to Wyatt*] What's happening as you listen?

> *Inviting a U-turn. "What's happening?" is a more effective U-turn invitation than asking, "How do you feel?"*

Wyatt: I'm honestly confused. I don't know what to do.

Therapist: You have a part who is trying hard to *do* something. Say more.

> Naming the part and its activity

Wyatt: Look, my feeling is that I'm always in trouble. There must be something else I'm supposed to do, right?

Therapist: What is the hope of the part who tries to *do* something?

> Fleshing out its hopes (or fears)

Wyatt: That I'll get it right and understand what's going on.

Therapist: So that Gwen will be happy? [*he nods*] And then what?

> Deepening the inquiry

Wyatt: [*after a long silence*] I don't know… She'll like me. I'll feel successful. I won't be a failure in her eyes.

Therapist: [*to Gwen*] Were you aware of this?

Gwen: Not exactly. Not what Wyatt is saying right now.

Therapist: [*to Gwen*] Would you like to know more?

Gwen: Yeah!

Therapist: [*to Gwen*] If Wyatt is available to do some exploration with me right now, are you available to listen?

> Looking for a genuine yes, where no parts are objecting

Gwen: I am.

Therapist: [*to Wyatt*] Would you be willing to do some exploring with me right now and get to know this part who feels like a failure?

Wyatt: Okay, I guess.

Therapist: [*to Wyatt*] Sounds like some parts have concerns. Let's check in with that before we go anywhere.

Wyatt: Oh well. I'm not fond of this "exploring parts" stuff.

Therapist: I understand. Let me reassure your wary parts. You are in charge here, and you get to say what you are available for. If you're willing to do this, we will check in regularly with your concerned parts, and they can interrupt at any time.

> Inviting protectors to stick around and do their job if they feel the need

Wyatt: That sounds good.

Therapist: [*to Gwen*] You have agreed to witness Wyatt's inquiry today. I want to check with you. Is that a genuine yes? Are there any parts who feel hesitant?

> *Helping activated parts in the listening partner to unblend*

Gwen: Yeah, I'm sure. I'm truly curious.

> *Listening for the "C" words that speak of the client's Self, like curiosity, caring, and compassion*

Therapist: [*to Gwen*] If you need help, I'm here.

> *Reassuring the client and offering ongoing help*

Therapist: [*continuing with Wyatt*] As I listened, I heard you speaking of many parts. A vigilant part who tries to take care of Gwen, a part who withdraws to avoid conflict, and a part who doesn't want to fail in Gwen's eyes.

> *Naming parts to differentiate them and support unblending*

Wyatt: Sounds right. I'm feeling defeated right now.

Therapist: What if we started right there? The defeated feeling.

Wyatt: It's heavy.

Therapist: Is it okay to focus on that? [*he nods*] Is the feeling familiar?

Wyatt: All my life. I try and try but never quite get things right. Except maybe parenting. I think I've done a good job with the kids. Oh, and I guess I've done okay in my career. But in relationships, I'm a loser.

Therapist: There's a judging part. It thinks you're a loser in your relationship with Gwen?

> *Naming inner shaming*

Wyatt: [*angrily*] Obviously Gwen thinks so. She complains enough.

> *Revealing his external shaming part (the "outer judge")*

Therapist: So there's a part who feels like you're a loser and a part who judges Gwen when you feel that way. Would these parts move back slightly so you can focus on the one who feels so bad?

Wyatt: Being pissed off feels better.

Therapist: That makes sense. Can I ask you a question? [*he nods*] Does it make sense that the parts who are judging you and Gwen are trying to protect you from feeling like a loser?

Wyatt: Sure! Who wants this?

Therapist: [*to Gwen*] Are you with us?

Gwen: I am.

Therapist: Okay, Wyatt, let's ask these judging parts if they are willing to soften and let you try something new.

(*Helping protectors unblend*)

Wyatt: [*closes his eyes*] I can feel that uncomfortable tension between just wanting to make sure Gwen is okay and wanting to withdraw from her.

Therapist: You spoke of those parts earlier. So here they are.

Wyatt: Yes.

Therapist: I can assure them that Gwen is doing fine. She's here with me feeling curious. Would they give you a little room so we can go on checking in with the judging parts?

Wyatt: Okay.

Therapist: Are they willing to let you try something new?

Wyatt: Reluctantly. Oh, okay. As long as they don't have to go away.

Therapist: What do you notice now?

Wyatt: A lump in my stomach. This is so familiar. My mother. Always needing something that she wasn't able to give herself. I was so overwhelmed. And where was my fucking father!

Therapist: Where was your father?

Wyatt: Just around being a bastard. He loved humiliating me. He was always envious!

Therapist: Here's a part who's angry with your father. Who needs your attention first? The angry one or the one who feels like a loser?

Wyatt: The loser.

Therapist: How are you feeling toward that part now?

(*Checking for blending*)

Wyatt: I feel sorry for him.

Therapist: In kindness or pity?

Wyatt: [*putting his face in his hands*] Some of both. [*the therapist turns toward Gwen to make eye contact*]

> *Staying connected with the partner throughout the session*

Gwen: This is so sad!

Therapist: [*to Wyatt*] Did you hear Gwen?

Wyatt: Yes. But I don't want pity.

Gwen: I don't pity you! I'm listening. Remember I knew your father well. He wanted to destroy you.

Gwen's statement at this point in the dialogue signaled that she was unblended and that her heart was open. This kind of active, attuned listening creates safety and deepens the process.

Wyatt: [*weeping*] Yes. Thank you. That helps. But I need to get out of this. [*his eyes are still tightly closed*] It's too much!

Therapist: We can take you out of this any time. But can we first check on who inside is feeling overwhelmed right now?

> *Providing reassurance and asking for permission*

Wyatt: All those parts we asked to wait.

Therapist: What's happening with them?

Wyatt: I'm so ashamed.

Therapist: If we could free that part from feeling shameful, would it help all your other parts?

Wyatt: It would be a huge relief.

Therapist: Okay. Do we have everyone's permission to do that?

Wyatt: Okay.

Therapist: What I heard, Wyatt, is that your mother put a lot of pressure on you to take care of her, while your father humiliated you. Did I get that right?

Wyatt: That's it exactly.

Therapist: Can you see the boy who was pressured and shamed in this way?

Wyatt: Yes.

Therapist: How do you feel toward him?

> *Checking for unblending*

Wyatt: I care about him.

Therapist: Is it okay to stay with him? [*Wyatt takes a big breath and nods*] How old is he?

Wyatt: Many ages.

Therapist: How far back can he take you?

Wyatt: To age three.

Therapist: Can you see the three-year-old? [*Wyatt nods*] Hear him? [*Wyatt nods*] Feel him?

Wyatt: I feel him.

Therapist: How do you feel toward him?

> (Checking for unblending again)

Wyatt: I'm open.

Therapist: What did he need back then from an adult that he didn't get? [*making eye contact with Gwen, who nods*]

> (Staying connected with the partner)

Wyatt: He needed to be a child, not a thing!

Therapist: Of course he did. Can you let him know you understand?

Wyatt: [*opens his eyes and looks at Gwen*] I am afraid of getting it wrong. I guess that makes sense. There was so much at risk. [*Gwen nods*]

Therapist: Stay with him a little longer if you can. [*Wyatt closes his eyes*] How does he respond to you?

Wyatt: He's glad I'm here.

Therapist: What did he come to believe about himself?

Wyatt: I get it. He felt all wrong and worthless.

Therapist: Is he ready to let that go? [*Wyatt nods*] What's happening in your body?

> (Checking for ANS activation)

Wyatt: I feel weirdly relaxed.

Therapist: Where is he now?

Wyatt: Well… he just wanted to be with me, so he got out of there. He's with me.

Therapist: Is he ready to let go of the burden of feeling wrong and worthless? [*Wyatt nods*] How would he like to do that?

Wyatt: [*weeping*] He's so young. I'm holding him just like I hold my boys. It's draining out of him. Is that okay?

Therapist: Is it okay with him?

Wyatt: Yes. It's good. That's good. He's good.

Therapist: What does he need now?

Wyatt: To sleep in my arms where he is safe. He just wants to *be*—you know be with me.

Therapist: How are the judgmental parts and that vigilant caretaker doing now?

Wyatt: Relaxed—for now.

Therapist: Would they like to have the opportunity tell their stories sometime?

Wyatt: I think so. Let's see.

Therapist: Yes. Let's see what they need. They can let you know. When it feels right, make your way back. Take your time.

ℌ

After Wyatt made loving contact with his wounded boy, the couple spent the rest of the session making sense of how chronic shaming in childhood had caused Wyatt to believe he was shameful, which led to his prominent coping strategies and affected their adult life together.

When the Therapist Makes a Relational Mistake*

Most clients are aware that the therapist is in a position of authority, which we define as the ability to influence and act as a resource (Barstow, 2005). In order to deserve authority, we need more than good intentions. We need to embrace our role with clarity, concern, and compassion. We need to understand the power differential within the therapeutic relationship and be sensitive to the ways in which our mistakes impact our clients (Barstow, 2005). All close relationships suffer misconnection, misattunement, wounding, and conflict, including the therapeutic relationship. Mishaps and mistakes are an inevitable part of being in a relationship.

Our job is to take responsibility for our role and our actions and make corrections as needed. We need to model how to restore trust, renew connection, and strengthen relationships. While mistakes are context dependent, some are common. Here are a few examples. The therapist has a part who:

- Engages the client's protectors in a power struggle
- Is misattuned for some reason and gets it wrong—and the client experiences empathic failure

---

* We thank Michele Bograd, PhD, for her contributions to the ideas and observations in this section. We have paraphrased some of her thinking throughout what follows.

- Commits a microaggression due to implicit bias
- Is not clear about something, like money, scheduling, or what they can and cannot provide
- Gets defensive when a client gives them feedback
- Talks about their own experience without getting permission from the client first
- Doesn't recognize that the therapeutic relationship is not mutual
- Fails to address erotic transference or countertransference appropriately

Even when we have positive intentions, we can have a negative impact on our clients. However, we are not likely to learn the true impact of our therapeutic interventions—and whether we have caused a relational rupture—unless the client's parts feel free to express themselves. We create this level of comfort by listening carefully, not defending ourselves, and staying curious about our impact. In addition, we need to be mindful of waiting to say what we really mean until after the client feels heard ("Is there more you want to speak for?") (Barstow, 2005) and the client's protectors have been willing to unblend.

Good interpersonal boundaries reduce the likelihood of mistakes and mitigate their impact when they do occur. Good boundaries create an atmosphere of safety and are essential for the therapeutic alliance. As the person with the most resources in the relationship, we are in charge of setting, communicating, and maintaining boundaries. Although our clients may help to create these boundaries and will have their own feelings and issues regarding boundaries, boundary maintenance is our job. For example:

Iris: My *no* has never meant *no* to anyone. I've been violated many times.

Therapist: Your *no* will mean *no* with me. We will explore any part who says *no* until we both understand its concerns and it feels safe here. I am very sincere about this. Deal?

Iris: Deal!

Even with positive intentions and good boundaries, though, relational mistakes can still impact the therapeutic relationship. Making repairs signals to the client that their safety is paramount, their reality is valid, and the power hierarchy is out in the open. Rather than making a quick apology—which can be used to avoid conflict and side-step difficult conversations—we have to own the mistake and make the repair sincere. By taking full responsibility for our actions without being defensive, self-deprecating, or placating the client, we model how to be congruent, present, and unblended. If the client has a part who tries to rescue you from a relational mistake, ask them to help fearful parts relax back so they can speak for any parts who feel angry, hurt, or confused. Mistakes can also, of course, activate our own critics to go on the attack internally. We may have a protective part who:

- Shames us for not being perfect, which interferes with our ability to stay interpersonally connected
- Activates in response to an exile's shamefulness internally and responds by getting angry with the client
- Believes admitting mistakes means we are a bad therapist
- Feels powerless when we are in a one-down position
- Fears that admitting to a mistake will lead to losing the client's respect and losing influence with the client

To overcome these challenges, we suggest making a commitment to exploring your parts going forward and forgiving any part who makes a mistake. In addition, making repairs is an ongoing process that promotes safety, so we ask clients to give us feedback on a regular basis. Finally, get consultation when you need it.

PHASE 3 OF TREATMENT: ENDING

In the last phase of IFIO, we help couples heal wounds and forgive betrayal, which all couples experience at some point. Some betrayals are small and mundane, like poor attunement. Others, like having an affair, can be very consequential. Repeated, unresolved injuries, great and small, cause protective parts to commit even more resources to guarding the heart. As the relationship erodes, the couple comes to view each other as adversaries rather than supports and resources. To recapture trust, they need a safe way to take responsibility for injurious behaviors. In this last phase of therapy, we unpack the experiences, feelings, and beliefs that couples often have regarding betrayal, apology, and forgiveness.

Repair

Oftentimes, individuals struggle to make amends because their protectors are holding onto a variety of distortions that block repair. For example, they may have protectors who associate the experience of apologizing with:

- Accepting undeserved or unbearable blame
    o "It takes two to tango. If I take full responsibility, I'll be letting her off the hook."
- Encouraging a variety of future dangers, especially being shamed
    o "When I say that I'm sorry, he uses it against me later."
- Being chronically deprived of validation in the past, so they insist on being correct now
    o "I'm right, so why should I apologize?"

When protectors promote these distortions, people tend to move on without hearing each other or without ever making a full, genuine repair. They may apologize badly, turn the table and blame the partner, dishonestly self-deprecate, or try to justify their hurtful behavior. Doing any of this will leave wounds festering and encourage the partner's vigilant protectors to raise the drawbridge. Repair is essential for maintaining intimacy, so in IFIO we challenge avoidant and prickly protectors to try something new. Specifically, we ask them to unblend and meet the Self. If they are not ready to do this, we listen and validate their concerns. But we don't listen passively. We keep asking for permission to present alternatives, and we keep promising that our offer will be of benefit to protectors, as well as exiles.

When making repairs, we help clients distinguish between shame and guilt. Although both emotions evoke feelings of self-consciousness, they are fundamentally different (Lewis, 1974). Shame involves negative global self-judgments (e.g., "I am bad"), whereas guilt focuses on accepting responsibility for a particular behavior (e.g., "I did wrong"). Although shame is associated with maladaptive, self-destructive behavior (e.g., avoidance, addiction, blame), guilt motivates us to repair and reconnect (e.g., "I transgressed, and I owe you an apology").

Historically, a lot of writing in the field of mental health has conflated guilt with shame, and many clients follow suit. We find that clients benefit a lot from understanding the difference between the two. Most of us have protective parts who will transgress in a pinch, and doing a U-turn helps us take responsibility for these parts and their actions. Guilt is a cue to assess whether and how we have transgressed. We do not want to reassure clients who feel appropriately guilty. Rather, we want to help them separate from extreme protectors, hear from the parts who feel guilty, care about the parts who transgressed, and take responsibility for their behavior, including by offering reparation to anyone who has been harmed.

We also don't want to reassure self-critical clients, mostly because doing so has little lasting effect. We all have shaming parts, and they will continue to do their jobs until the underlying parts who feel shameful (i.e., the exiles) are more securely attached to the client's Self and feel better. With this goal, we challenge critical protectors to allow the client's Self to care for exiles in the usual way: helping extreme protectors unblend, having compassion for them, and inviting them to notice their effect on each other and on other people. When a protector can register guilt, the client can make a genuine repair.

Forgiveness

From an IFIO perspective, forgiveness takes time and is different for everyone. It's a process of helping protectors let go so clients can feel sad, grieve, and move on with an open heart. It does *not* involve condoning harmful behavior, letting someone "off the hook" for harmful behavior, ignoring boundaries, or staying in a relationship despite repeated injury. As clients cultivate compassion and come to hold themselves with tenderness, it grows easier to forgive and mend betrayal. However, the more polarized and mistrusting their protectors are, the longer this will take and the more difficult it will be.

Couples who come to therapy after a serious betrayal are often either in a state of collapse (e.g., compliance, withdrawal, depression) or activation (e.g., anger, revenge), or some combination of the two. Underneath the collapse or anger, we find confusion and unhealed injuries from earlier in life. As a result, the first step in forgiveness involves promising protectors that we will focus first on finding vulnerable exiles and helping them not to overwhelm. Then, gently and respectfully, we explore what forgiveness means to each partner personally and to the couple. If protectors allow the Self to access and heal exiles, then their urges to avoid, deny, or take revenge deflate, and partners can grieve.

However, many partners have protectors who fear forgiveness and associate it with unlikely outcomes, such as forgetting the past (e.g., "You mean forgive and forget? I don't want to forget!") and being more vulnerable after having forgiven (e.g., "If I forgive this behavior, then it will happen again. I'll be a sitting duck"). Additionally, protectors sometimes associate forgiveness with alarming outcomes. For example, vengeful parts have to be convinced that it's safe to let go of the idea of retributive justice (e.g., "You're asking me to let him get away with this. He should suffer too!"), angry parts have to relinquish the physically inflating and emotionally distracting effects of righteousness (e.g., "If I forgive her, I just know I'll get depressed"), and vigilant parts have to let go of the fear that the client is a child without resources (e.g., "If I don't protect her, who will?").

Raising the topic of forgiveness smokes out parts who need reassurance, as well as parts who need help but have remained hidden from view. When the repair process begins, we can predict that partners have shaming parts and parts who feel shameful, and we also need to remember that not every couple sees betrayal the way we do. Every therapist who works with betrayal must be mindful of their own experiences and views on betrayal, especially infidelity. As the therapist, ask yourself:

- What are my beliefs about betrayal?
- How do I view the wounding partner?
- How do I view the wounded partner?
- Are extramarital affairs a symptom, an attempted cure, or neither?
- Does it make a difference to me how the disclosure happened?

Be prepared for your own polarizations to show up when a couple begins to unpack a serious betrayal. In addition, take care to avoid these common mistakes:

- Focusing on the years of discontent or initiating intimacy building before addressing the breach in trust
- Not describing your approach to the repair process with the couple
- Allowing the wounded partner's outraged protectors to blend and dominate the therapy for too long
- Allowing the wounding partner to blame the wounded partner for past transgressions or ask the wounded partner to take responsibility prematurely
- Pushing forgiveness
- Blending with parts of your own who have an agenda and cause you to lose track of what the couple wants and needs

BETRAYAL, REPAIR, AND FORGIVENESS

Therapists can ask the following IFIO questions to facilitate the last phase of therapy:

- "How are you feeling right now?"
- "What do each of you hope for?"
- "What would a successful outcome look like?"
    - o Listen to their parts.
    - o Gauge how motivated each partner is toward repair at this moment.
- "Have you done repair work with a therapist, a coach, or each other?"
- "Is the behavior ongoing?" (or "Has the affair stopped?")
- "Have you talked about this? How did it go?"
- "How was this disclosed?"

The IFIO Method with Repair and Forgiveness

Many couples have no blueprint for repairing ruptures, small or large. A conflict or betrayal that isn't mended will ulcerate and burden their relationship, resulting in less trust and less heartfelt connection. The seven steps of repair outlined in this section can be used for all betrayals, big and small, including mundane infractions. A repair can take minutes or years, depending on the couple. The meaning that protective parts hold about the past and the other person, as well as their fear of being hurt and humiliated, are what make apology and forgiveness difficult. But even when partners decide to part ways, forgiving and loving their own parts as well as apologizing to and forgiving each other are transformative.

Although a heartfelt repair can come in many forms, the seven steps presented here focus on increasing each partner's ability to speak for their parts, listen from the heart, empathize with each other's pain, and take responsibility for harmful actions (Herbine-Blank et al. 2016; Springs 2004). While these seven steps are effective for ruptures that range from relational aches and pains to serious betrayals, couples move through them at their own pace, sometimes in a circular rather than a linear fashion, because the process can evoke shame and many parts may need attention along the way. Before leading couples through the seven steps, help the couple by reviewing how the internal system works with a few specific assertions:

- We do not control our parts.
- Our parts can control us when they blend with us.
- Helping parts be willing to unblend is key to being in relationship with them, which is key to progress in therapy.
- We have many parts, and we are vastly more than our most extreme parts.
- Regardless of the cost to others and us, extreme parts view their behavior as protective, essential, and largely non-negotiable.
    - Proactive protectors (managers) are always trying to manage both external and internal relationships. Despite the costs of their behavior, their intentions are good.
    - Reactive protectors (firefighters) focus on rapid internal change and have little concern about external consequences. That is, even if their behavior is destructive, their intentions are good—but just for us, not for others.
- We can get to know, understand, and help all extreme parts. They are misguided but not bad.
- We can forgive ourselves fully by taking full responsibility for the actions of our parts.
- Once our protective parts trust us, we can help them by offering to solve their problem, which is the underlying imperative of warding off emotional pain.

In addition, therapists should emphasize the following important assertions about the process and nature of forgiveness. First, individuals can have contradictory ideas about forgiveness. That is, their parts can disagree. In addition, forgiveness does not involve forgetting, nor does it change the transgressor's responsibility for consequences. It does not let anyone off the hook. Rather, forgiving requires that clients exhibit compassion for themselves and their partner. When clients release their anger and resentment in the process of forgiving, they heal and benefit directly.

Once therapists have reviewed these assertions regarding IFS and forgiveness, they are ready to introduce the seven steps of repair. Although we summarize these steps here, we have illustrated them throughout the manual:

1. **Creating safety for both partners.** In the beginning, the therapist should avoid content in favor of process and never take sides on polarizing issues. Reassure the couple that you can help them both with all types of feelings (e.g., anger, hurt, betrayal, fear, shame).

2. **Speaking for parts and listening from the heart.** Explain that you aim to help them with internal and external shaming by establishing a new way of speaking and listening. Then teach them to unblend so they can speak on behalf of their parts and listen from the heart.

3. **Taking full responsibility by means of self-inquiry and self-forgiveness.** At the outset, the wounded partner is the listener and the wounding partner is the speaker. The wounded partner (the listener) helps their parts unblend so they can listen from the heart. The wounding partner (the speaker) notices parts who have caused harm, as well as the parts who shame them internally for having caused harm, and does a U-turn by helping harming parts (and shaming parts when necessary) unblend. Next, partners switch roles. The wounding partner now listens (from the heart, with help if needed), asking for time to help shaming protectors who activate internally as needed. The wounded partner (now the speaker) also helps protectors unblend and speaks for them about the impact of the wounding partner's behavior.

4. **Reconciling.** To give a sincere apology, the wounding partner—who is now unblended from extreme parts—responds to the wounded partner's impact statement. If their response is shame-based (e.g., "I'm so bad"), the wounding partner's protectors need more help. However, if the response is guilt-based, we know the wounding partner feels genuine remorse for their behavior and their protectors are willing to change. Throughout this process, the wounded partner listens.

5. **Setting an intention.** The wounding partner details their plan to help their parts. The wounded partner listens.

6. **Forgiving.** At this point, we explore the wounded partner's willingness to receive an apology and consider forgiveness. We do not push or pressure the wounded partner to forgive. If the wounded partner refuses to forgive, the other is likely to feel they are being asked to beg for mercy in perpetuity. In this case, we help the unforgiven partner do a U-turn, unblend from reactive parts, and attend to their exiles so they can respond to this outcome in a Self-led way.

7. **Acknowledging unique historical experiences while sharing responsibility.** If the wounded partner does not believe they share responsibility for the conflict, we help them do a U-turn so they can listen to their parts, whose skewed views on responsibility are rooted in history.

Ultimately, we want partners to see their relationship as a co-creation based on the needs of certain exiled parts. The therapy process helps each partner meet the needs of their exiled parts so they can recreate their external relationship on a foundation of mutual curiosity and respect. The wounded partner, however, must be ready for a conversation about mutual responsibility. Depending on how egregious the injury, this can take a long time.

BETRAYAL AND REPAIR

The following case example illustrates the beginning of how we introduce a couple to the process of repair following betrayal. Bob and Judith, a cisgendered, heterosexual, European-American couple in their mid-sixties, had been married for 32 years. Their children were grown. They sought therapy to decide if their marriage could be salvaged after Bob had a series of affairs. The following is an excerpt from their second session with an IFIO therapist.

Therapist: Welcome, I want to hear from both of you about last week's session and how the week went. Who would like to start?

Judith: [*looking at Bob*] Why don't you start for a change?

Bob: I'd prefer not to.

Therapist: [*to Bob*] You prefer not to speak? Can you tell me a little more about that?

Bob: [*lowers his head and sighs*] It doesn't feel safe.

Therapist: I hear you. It doesn't feel safe to speak right now—

Judith: [*interrupting*] But it is safe to have affairs and engage in myriad other bad behaviors?

Therapist: Judith, I am going to interrupt you. A moment ago, you said you would like to hear from Bob. So I'll have a conversation with him, and then the three of us can decide what will be most helpful today. How does that sound?

(*Redirecting firmly and reframing*)

Judith: Okay, yes. Thank you. It would be helpful for somebody to have a conversation with him.

Therapist: Bob, last week I introduced the idea of parts. [*he nods*] What I hear is that you have a part who is afraid.

Bob: Many parts of me are afraid!

Therapist: Could you speak for that fear?

Bob: It always ends up in a fight, so it's better not to speak.

Therapist: That is what you hear yourself saying to yourself? "I am safer if I don't speak"?

Bob: Yes. And that's my pattern too.

Therapist: The pattern is you stay quiet?

Bob: Right.

Therapist: And since you are becoming more aware of your pattern, are you also aware of what happens inside Judith when you don't speak?

Bob: She gets mad.

Therapist: Okay. I'm hearing that some of your parts feel unsafe if you speak, but then Judith gets mad, so there's no win for you. Am I getting it right?

Bob: You are.

Therapist: We'll return to your dilemma, but right now I'm going to check in with Judith. [*to Judith*] What's happening for you?

Judith: I feel hopeless. I'll never get what I want or need.

Therapist: If I'm hearing you right, you're in touch with parts who feel sad and hopeless. But you're less in touch with the anger you spoke for last week?

Judith: To tell the truth, I'm mostly angry. It's safer that way.

Therapist: That makes sense. But in this moment, you are also in touch with hopelessness and despair and the belief that you will never get what you want or need from Bob.

(*Validating and reflecting back*)

Judith: That's right. That's exactly right.

Therapist: Bob, what happens in you when you hear this?

Bob: I feel like it's just better to get out of here. She may be sad or whatever, but she's waiting to unload years of anger and resentment. I've heard it so many times, I'm not available to hear it again.

Therapist: And that makes sense to me as well.

> *Validating, which supports unblending*

Bob: Thank you for that.

Therapist: I understand from last week that you, Judith, have a part who gets understandably angry and that you, Bob, have a part who understandably turns away. And I hear that you, Judith, have been experiencing Bob's distancing—among other things—for years.

Judith: Thank you for that. Yes, among other things! There's a lot of history here.

Therapist: While both of you have parts who want to be heard and understood, this impasse I'm hearing about right now is what actually happens. Anger and hopelessness with an inability to have the conversations you really need to have. Am I getting this right? [*they nod*]

> *Checking for accuracy and using parts language*

Therapist: [*continuing*] I know you are coming to see me after seeing several other therapists, and I want to ask once more, what is the hope of trying therapy again?

> *Listening to the hopes of the parts who made the decision to come to therapy*

Bob: I'm not sure. I guess I still hope something might change.

Therapist: What would that be?

> *Looking for clarity that will help this phase of therapy move forward*

Bob: I don't really know. Maybe it would be like getting past all the anger to something that looks like a relationship?

Therapist: And when you say, "the anger," do you mean your anger as well as Judith's?

Bob: Oh yes.

Therapist: Bob, I hear you acknowledging that you, too, are angry and that this impasse involves a back and forth of anger and resentment. You have parts who pull you in different ways, including into affairs.

Bob: Yes, that's true.

Therapist: And Judith, what is your hope for trying therapy again?

Judith: My hope is that he would stop the affairs and all the things he does that tell me he doesn't love me.

Therapist: I hear that you wish Bob would do things differently, and you wish to feel loved by him. And I am also aware of parts who are willing to try therapy with yet another therapist. If this could be successful, what outcome would you want for yourself or for the relationship?

Judith: I want to see if we want to be together.

Therapist: I'm curious. [*looking from one to the other*] Between the time you sat down here and now, what has been happening in your bodies? What are you experiencing?

Checking for ANS regulation and unblending

Judith: [*a long sigh*] I'm calmer, less tense. [*pauses*] I think I can actually hear more of what you're saying. I was so upset when I sat down that I couldn't concentrate. I wonder if you are trying to figure out if you can help us?

Therapist: I believe I can help you.

Judith: So you're wondering if we want help?

Therapist: Exactly. I'm guessing, Judith, that as you're feeling a little calmer, your brain is able to take in and process more information?

Judith: True.

Bob: I notice something just shifted a little in me. I feel a tiny bit hopeful. It feels very risky to say, but I do. I'm also wondering if Judith will take responsibility for her part of what's wrong with our relationship.

Therapist: Bob, I want to slow down for a moment and be curious about what just happened. First, I heard you take a risk and say something very vulnerable. Then, right after that, I heard another part say something about Judith.

Bob: So I have done a lot of things in this relationship that have been really hurtful. I admit it, but I am not the only one.

Therapist: So you don't want to be the only bad one. Is that right?

Bob: That's exactly right.

Therapist: And I think I'm hearing that you have a part who believes you're the bad one.

> *Returning to parts language*

Bob: Most definitely.

Therapist: And what's that like, to feel like the bad one?

Bob: Not fun.

Therapist: And is that part here right now?

Bob: Yes, I feel it all over. Very shameful.

Therapist: And does it make sense that even as you experience one part's shamefulness, another part wants to distract you and make sure Judith shares the discomfort? [*Bob pauses to think, then nods*]

> *Pointing out the pairing of protectors with exiles*

Therapist: [*continuing*] So I want to reassure those parts. If you choose to continue couple therapy with me, we will eventually get into the entire history of your relationship. But for this moment, I want to stay with what's happening here and now. [*turns to Judith*] What's happening for you as you listen?

Judith: [*a long pause*] I'm trying to believe what Bob is saying. He wants me to take responsibility, but I want him to take responsibility. He acknowledges that he has done a lot to damage our relationship.

Therapist: What is it like in this moment to hear Bob acknowledge that he has hurt you?

Judith: It's good and bad. On the one hand, the acknowledgment feels good. On the other hand, it just brings up all that hurt and anger. I don't like thinking or hearing about it. The affairs, the other women...

Therapist: It sounds, Bob, like you have made some choices, affairs being one of them, that have been very hurtful. I'm curious if any other therapies have offered to help you repair that damage?

Bob: [*shakes his head*] Maybe, but I don't remember it.

Judith: I don't even know what you're talking about. What are you talking about?

Therapist: I'll tell you what I believe. When a betrayal leaves one person feeling deeply hurt, the injury needs to be healed before they can think about what was happening in the relationship before the betrayal. I believe this is critical.

Judith: We haven't heard this before. [*looking at Bob*] Not that I remember.

Bob: Me neither. But it makes sense. [*sighs*]

Therapist: Can you tell me about that sigh, Bob?

Bob: Well, maybe you can handle us! Maybe you can actually help.

Therapist: So maybe I can sit with all the hurt and be present to the suffering in your relationship and help you heal?

Judith: What you offer is clearly different. There has been damage. We do need repair.

> *Note the passive voice—Judith is not ready to consider her role in any damage*

Therapist: Repair is an optimistic goal, and I'd like to tell you a little about the repair process I use.

> *Offering to give them a brief description of the IFIO repair process*

Judith: That would be good.

Bob: Yes, I would like to hear that.

Therapist: I expect you will have some difficult conversations, but I can teach you a new way of speaking and listening to each other so you don't fall into shaming and blaming, or collapsing and running away. I can teach you to speak for your parts and listen from the heart. For you, Bob, this will involve listening as Judith describes the impact of your affairs. And I will keep the process as safe as possible. I would want you to be able to empathize with Judith, feel remorse, and discover what Judith needs in order to heal. Your inquiry would include looking at and taking responsibility for the choices your parts made on your behalf, as well as understanding and addressing their motivations. And you, Judith. You have parts who are very angry, hurt, humiliated, hopeless, and scared. Am I right?

Judith: You are so right. I feel all those things. But when I start feeling too vulnerable, I rage. It's better.

Therapist: I understand that raging feels empowering. My approach with parts who need that would be somewhat different. I would want you to be able to express every feeling you have but to do it in a way that Bob can hear. His parts need to understand their impact and be willing to hand the reins back to him so he can take responsibility and make repairs.

Judith: That's what I want too! Part of the raging is to make sure he gets that. I believe he hasn't gotten it yet.

Therapist: As long as his parts are defending against your rage, I'm not sure he can truly hear you.

Judith: [*long pause*] I don't really want to help him out. But I do want something to shift. Nothing else has worked. So I am going to go with your idea.

Therapist: Great. And I will be here to help you all along the way. Both of you.

> *Letting them know the plan and offering ongoing help*

Judith: Knowing that you will help us along the way makes my whole body relax.

Bob: Mine too.

Judith: [*turning to Bob*] I need to know that you won't have any more affairs. If you do, I'll leave.

Bob: [*looking at Judith*] I do understand this, Judith.

Therapist: Once things begin to shift, we can work on reconciliation and forgiveness.

Judith: [*puts up her hands*] Oh, I'm not ready to forgive!

Therapist: That makes sense to me. We'll discuss forgiveness later, if and when you're both ready. There will be no pressure about forgiving. Right now, we'll focus on changing your conversation and work toward a sincere repair.

> *Alleviating any pressure to forgive*

Therapist: [*continuing*] I notice you're looking at Bob.

Judith: I'm curious if he agrees with what you're saying.

Bob: Doing something different would be good.

Judith: So we agree on something! [*Bob nods and Judith laughs*] We agree! Wow.

Therapist: I appreciate you wanting to do something different. I know this has been hard, and you wonder what more could shift.

Bob: I'll be honest. This scares me. I am willing to give it a try, but I don't know if I can do it. I still don't want to be the target of all blame and anger.

Therapist: Of course you don't. But when I said some of these conversations will involve listening to the impact of your behavior on Judith, you did nod.

Bob: Yes. And I also want Judith to hear me about how some of her choices early in our relationship affected me. Like her anger.

Therapist: Of course Judith has hurt some of your parts over the 32 years of your marriage.

Bob: [*teary*] This is the first time anyone has acknowledged that. It's powerful. Thank you.

Therapist: And I believe this rupture in the present needs to be healed before we explore all the ways you have hurt each other over the course of your marriage. Does what I'm proposing make sense?

Bob: I get that, absolutely.

Therapist: Would you be willing to say what you get, right now, directly to Judith?

> *Reinforcing moments of connection when the opportunity arises*

Bob: [*inhales sharply*] That's scary. [*looks at Judith*] I know if we're going to get anywhere, I have to hear what you feel about what I did. And I have to take much more responsibility.

Therapist: What's it like to hear that, Judith?

Judith: [*pauses*] I have goosebumps. [*looks at Bob*] It's a game changer. I never heard you say anything like that. Is it real?

Bob: It's real.

⁂

Needless to say, this was just the beginning. Bob began individual therapy and got to know the parts who chose to have affairs in response to his loneliness, anger toward Judith, and loss of joy in his life. Over time, he understood how his inner dilemmas and his childhood trauma had contributed to this behavior, and he was able to listen to Judith without defending himself. Once he became more hopeful, believing he could heal, and their relationship could survive, he was able to apologize to Judith with genuine remorse.

Over time, as Judith experienced the power of speaking for her devastated parts without raging, she gained trust in herself and was able to be curious about what had led to Bob feeling so resentful and hostile toward her earlier in their relationship. However, until they were less reactive, and their relationship was kinder and gentler—with more moments of connection and fun—the topic of forgiveness was off the table. Therapists can use the following handouts with clients in order to learn and practice repair processes, which are a critical step in unburdening from past hurts and betrayals, healing relationships, and reclaiming trust.

THE IFIO DO-OVER:
Catch Your Protector in Action and Try Again

A *do-over* is a quick repair. As we befriend protectors and become aware of harm they have caused, it gets easier to notice when we are misattuned or unkind to our partner and interrupt the cycle by apologizing and asking to *redo* the interaction in a Self-led way. We outline the steps of a communication *do-over* here:

1. Acknowledge your misattunement or unkindness.

2. Ask your partner if they will stay with you so you can *redo* the communication.

3. Wait for their agreement.

4. Try again by speaking *for* your part, and then take time to notice and speak for the part's underlying (exiled) need.

5. Check in with your partner. What do they hear from their parts?

6. Listen from the Self.

Here is an example:

1. A frustrated part takes aim: "I've asked you over and over not to do that!"

2. The do-over: "I'm sorry I lashed out. I don't want to talk like that. May I try again?"

3. Wait for partner's affirmative response.

4. Then: "I have a part who feels frustrated when this happens repeatedly. I wonder if we could talk about the pattern at some point?"

5. Check in: "Did that land differently for you? Is there anything you want to say?"

6. Listen to the impact of your behavior without defensiveness.

Copyright © 2021, Toni Herbine-Blank, Martha Sweezy, *Internal Family Systems Couple Therapy Skills Manual*. All rights reserved.

3 Relational Neurobiology in IFIO

NEUROBIOLOGY AND EARLY LIFE EXPERIENCES[*]

In utero and during infancy (i.e., approximately the first 18 months of life), the brain experiences, learns, and "remembers" only through perception, sensation, emotion, and a sense of "knowing." Because infants have not yet developed the capacity for language, the brain has no storytellers at this developmental phase, which means our earliest memories are nonverbal and don't follow a linear storyline. Memories that form at this stage are known as implicit memories (Badenoch, 2008; Siegel, 1999). Around 18 months of age, we begin to acquire language and develop a form of autobiographical memory called explicit memory. With this new cognitive ability, our parts start telling stories and "making sense" of implicit learning that ascends into awareness.

During the early, implicit-memory-only phase of life, a child's attachment style develops in their interactions with parents and other caregivers. That is, early relational experiences form a template upon which children base all future relationships (Schore & Schore, 2007). When these early relational experiences are suboptimal and challenge the child's basic needs and sense of safety, long-term changes to brain circuits involved in emotion regulation, self-soothing, and social relatedness can result. Additionally, deficits in early caretaking affect the child's ability to regulate their ANS and self-soothe when they are afraid, which impairs their ability to attune and make connections with other people (Cozolino, 2006). This child is at risk of developing an insecure attachment style—they might be predominantly avoidant, or they might crave attention and fear it both at once—which continues into adulthood.

A person's unconscious, implicit memories of childhood wounds are stored in the amygdala, which is a primitive part of the brain that is deeply affected by social and emotional experiences early in life. When a present experience evokes emotional baggage from the past in the form of an implicit memory, that old experience can wash through the body as if it is happening in the here and now (Badenoch, 2008). The amygdala believes there is a threat in real time, and the body's ANS activates, turning off our capacity for rational thinking. As long as the present is subsumed by the past, stressful interactions can easily toss individuals back in time—but they won't be aware of what's happening.

As Bonnie Badenoch wrote in *Being a Brain-Wise Therapist*, "So many couples are locked in a pattern of shifting into dysregulation, either toward disengagement and deadness or hyperarousal and chaos. When they see how these patterns have been engrained through lack of parental responsiveness, they can begin to develop a soothing, mindful awareness of their own state and that of their partner, immediately increasing regulation. Being able to let go of blaming the other for these disruptions makes room for mutual compassion" (2008, p. 282).

---

[*]We thank John Palmer, IFIO trainer, for his guidance in writing this chapter about neuroscience and couple therapy.

To put this in parts language, when clients' young exiles blend, they feel overwhelmed with sensory information from the past, which sends the inner system a terribly discouraging message: The past will never end. When deeply shaming attachment injuries are superimposed onto present interactions and the past feels relentlessly duplicated in the present, protectors naturally believe that their extreme views and vigilance are justified. As a result, couples fight relentlessly over who said or did what to whom. The irony is that their recall will never be accurate because both implicit learning and stress hormones distort explicit memory.

Since therapists can't know with certainty what someone said or did during high-stress moments, there is no point in helping couples try to decipher what "really" happened. While a protector's need for validation makes sense, we validate its feelings and confusion, but not strategies that cause further harm. Protectors get clarity and relief when the exile's original experience is witnessed, and enough healing takes place to jettison shaming beliefs (e.g., "I'm unlovable").

We guide partners to break the habit of sparring over what really happened by introducing them to better alternatives, especially by helping them understand their neurobiology and by practicing unblending. In the process, we validate the good intentions of extreme protectors without endorsing their distorted views and guide partners in practicing new behaviors that change neurobiology, nourish confidence, and heal relationships. In couple therapy, secure attachments knit (or reknit) when the partner (outside) and the Self (inside) are available to extend kindness, attention, genuine curiosity, mature empathy, and loving compassion to wounded parts.

THE POLYVAGAL THEORY AND CO-REGULATION

The early view of the ANS posited that the nervous system comprised two branches—the sympathetic and parasympathetic branches—which served to activate and calm the body, respectively. However, Stephen Porges expanded this view with the Polyvagal Theory (2007), which maintains that the nervous system has three branches that constantly respond to relational conditions and work together in a hierarchical fashion.

On the one hand, we have the *sympathetic nervous system*; on the other, we have the *parasympathetic nervous system*, which comprises a dorsal vagal branch and a ventral vagal branch. The sympathetic nervous system responds to cues of danger by triggering the fight-or-flight response, which mobilizes the body for action. In contrast, the dorsal vagus and ventral vagus are both parts of the parasympathetic nervous system. The *dorsal vagus* is an evolutionarily older branch of the parasympathetic nervous system. It responds to cues of extreme danger with freeze or collapse behaviors (Dana, 2018). In IFIO, we would say that protective parts who operate in synchrony with the dorsal vagal system numb or freeze us, taking us out of connection and awareness, signaling their sense that extreme protection is in order.

Conversely, the *ventral vagus*, which is a more recent parasympathetic pathway, responds to cues of safety and promotes social connection. In IFIO, we theorize that a ventral vagal state facilitates Self-leadership.

Polyvagal Theory also posits two concepts of particular relevance for couples: neuroception and co-regulation. Neuroception refers to the unconscious process by which we are constantly scanning the external environment for cues of safety or danger. Rather than being logical or verbal, neuroception is a somatic, emotional, and associative process. In neuroception, the amygdala matches current experiences with prior experiences relevant to safety, which causes the ANS to react with relaxation or activation.

Subsequently, the left hemisphere makes up a story about what is happening, and this narrative is informed by the degree to which someone is led by their parts or their Self. When individuals are parts-led, the ANS is more likely to be in charge and the past has a greater influence over the storyline. In contrast, when individuals are Self-led, they can slow down, evaluate the accuracy of their reaction, check with their partner regarding their experience, and choose whether to respond and how to act wisely.

According to Polyvagal Theory, connecting with others provides us with the neuroception of safety, and it is through the formation of trusting relationships that we can co-regulate into a ventral vagal state. Co-regulation involves the reciprocal regulation of our ANS in connection with others. It creates a reassuring platform that signals safety and promotes further attachment. When a couple can co-regulate their nervous systems, they experience the pleasure of a self-reinforcing, co-created connection (Dana, 2018).

Importantly, a couple's concept of reciprocity in their relationship—the healthy, mutual give-and-take of support, love, and understanding—gives us more information about their dynamics and helps assess their ability to co-regulate in moments of stress (Dana, 2018). Of course, the reciprocity of giving in a couple will differ over time. In IFIO, we help partners keep noticing and assessing their ability to reciprocate.

NEUROBIOLOGY IN IFIO

We help couples by:

- Educating them on the ANS and normalizing their experience
- Teaching them to unblend from parts and helping each partner witness their relational trauma, which provides a contradictory, corrective experience for their exiles
- Giving the couple a disconfirming, reparative experience as they witness each other from the Self and hold compassion for their partner's wounds
- Providing education about the unconscious process of neuroception
- Using top-down/bottom-up interventions (Anderson, Sweezy, & Schwartz, 2017)
- Educating partners about co-regulation and reciprocity and conducting in-office exercises so partners can experience both
- Noticing co-regulation when it occurs spontaneously in the office between partners and enhancing the moment as much as possible

REGULATING THE AUTONOMIC NERVOUS SYSTEM

The following vignette illustrates self-regulation and co-regulation experiments to help a European-American couple, Dan and Cate, regulate their ANS in session. Dan is a transgender man who transitioned in his late twenties, and Cate is a cisgendered female who identifies as queer. They have been married for five years and together for seven. They sought couple therapy because both were reacting intensely to real or perceived threats in conversation, after which repair and reconnection were proving difficult.

Therapist: How was your week? And what will be helpful for today's session?

Dan: We just do not get along. I can never get anything right. I'm always in the doghouse with Cate.

Cate: Yes! Everything is about you, by the way. What about me? I have needs too, Dan!

Dan: See? We're off and running! [*he rolls his eyes*]

Therapist: Okay. You say the two of you are struggling to get along, Dan. You have a part who feels it can't do anything right. And you, Cate, spoke of parts with unmet needs. These issues are causing friction in your relationship. And both of you feel frustrated. Have I got all that right?

Dan: Yes.

Cate: That's right!

Therapist: This is just where we left off last time, so let's continue. [*Dan nods*]

Cate: [*to Dan*] You're always angry and yelling, by the way. I can't deal with that.

Dan: You're so damn condescending—who wouldn't be angry?

Therapist: Let's take a minute to notice what's happening right now. Start with your bodies. Take a few deep breaths. [*after a moment*] I want to remind you about your nervous systems. Are you fighting, fleeing, or freezing right now?

Cate: Okay. I have a part that's fleeing big time. I can hear its voice saying, "Get me out of here!"

Dan: And I'm in my usual place—itching for a fight.

Therapist: And what's happening in your body right now?

Dan: I'm cranking up. I'm tight. I can't help it.

Therapist: Got it, Dan. You're angry and getting more agitated. And you don't feel like you can help yourself. Does that sound right?

(*Mirroring*)

Dan: Right.

Therapist: [*turning to Cate*] And your body?

Cate: I'm tense, but it's not like I am going to get up and run. Not now anyway. Breathing deeply helps.

Therapist: Great. If you can keep noticing your body and your parts, I want to spend a little time with Dan.

Cate: Fine with me.

Therapist: [*to Dan*] All this energy in your body makes sense to me. It sounds like you're feeling unsafe? Can you look at me?

(*Offering co-regulation through eye contact and tone of voice*)

Therapist: [*continuing*] I have heard from you, Dan, that when you feel offended or threatened, you can get very angry, and the anger takes over your body. And sometimes it's hard for this angry part to unblend, as we say in IFS. It's hard to get yourself to the calm zone. And given your history, this makes complete sense to me. Is there more you want to say right now about how you're feeling?

> *Validation and mirroring followed by an invitation to say more about feelings*

Dan: I'm a little better. But I feel angry. Really angry.

Therapist: You are really angry.

> *Focusing on his feeling state*

Dan: Right.

Therapist: And you see the anger as a part?

Dan: I do.

Therapist: Where do you feel this part in or around your body?

> *Bringing awareness back to the body*

Dan: My chest.

Therapist: How do you feel toward it?

> *Checking for unblending*

Dan: I feel like I *am* him. He's all there is right now.

Therapist: Can I speak to him?

> *Getting permission for direct access*

Dan: Fine.

Therapist: [*turning to Cate*] Are you with us?

> *Staying connected with the partner*

Cate: I am. I feel more relaxed knowing you are with Dan and his anger.

Therapist: [*using direct access*] So I'll talk to Dan's angry part. Can you hear me? [*Dan nods*] Can you help me understand what's going on?

Dan: [*the angry part answers directly*] You don't understand what a weak, sniveling, incapable, spineless person Dan is! I am his only hope of staying alive.

Therapist: I see. You are strong and powerful?

Dan: [*the angry part*] He's alive, isn't he? He would probably be dead if it weren't for me. No one—and I mean no one—is going to threaten him ever again.

Therapist: And that includes those parts of Cate?

Dan: [*looks at Cate*] I guess it does.

Therapist: [*to Dan's Self*] Are you listening, Dan?

Dan: I am.

Therapist: How are you feeling toward this part now?

> Checking for unblending

Dan: I recognize these words. I started saying this in my teens.

Therapist: You have a part who started protecting you in this way back then?

Dan: Yes. And it's all true. I might be dead without this part.

Therapist: What's happening in your body right now?

> Checking his level of arousal

Dan: I feel calmer. But I still feel a lot of energy coursing around.

Therapist: I hear you. Lots of energy in your body. Can you handle it?

> Checking for unblending and getting permission to continue

Dan: I can.

Therapist: Are you available for more inquiry with this protective part?

Dan: I can try. The more I notice him, the more he changes. He was a lion, now he looks like a teenager.

Therapist: Does that make sense, or do you need to ask him about it?

Dan: No. It makes sense.

Therapist: When it feels right, please ask him whom he protects.

Dan: [*long pause*] Oh GOD! I don't want to go there.

Therapist: Because?

Dan: It's girl part. A young girl. Confused, terrorized.

Therapist: Who is afraid right now?

Dan: [*raises his voice*] Everyone is afraid of this girl! Do you not get this?

Therapist: Dan, I very much want to get this. What are they afraid of?

Dan: I will not be dragged back into the past. I left all that behind.

Therapist: So you have parts who feel threatened by her?

Dan: Yes.

Therapist: Visiting the past feels dangerous? I'm hearing that you have a part who is still trying to protect her, and you also have parts who want to exile her. Is that right?

> Naming the polarized protectors regarding this exile

Dan: That's exactly right.

Therapist: Can you feel this dilemma in your body?

Dan: So incredibly much anxiety!

Therapist: We're going to help all these parts, Dan. But first I'm going to check in with Cate. [*Dan nods, and the therapist turns to Cate*] Are you staying present? Does any of this make sense to you?

Cate: Yeah. It's funny. I sensed this somehow. Something is being pushed down all the time. And Dan acts like I am a threat. I can be an asshole, but I'm not going to beat him up or anything.

Dan: [*looks up sharply and snaps*] Well it feels like you are! You criticize me constantly.

Therapist: What just happened, Dan?

Dan: The anger came back.

Therapist: Do you notice how quickly this part deploys when it feels you're being threatened? [*Dan nods*] And if we could do something to help this giant protector feel safer, would he need to react to Cate this quickly?

> Inviting the part to receive support and be less reactive so the client has more choice in responding

Dan: It's true this part feels like he has no choice when he responds. So how would we change that?

Therapist: We continue to help you understand three important things. First, this is a protector who activates without your conscious awareness—that is, without your permission. He takes over your body. Second, your reaction makes complete sense given your childhood. And, third, this part is operating on the assumption that Cate is more dangerous than she really is. Since all this is true, we have several ways for you to help him unblend and regulate your nervous system, including healing the part this teenage boy protects.

> *Explaining the autonomic responses to perceived danger and the body's way of coping, and then offering an alternative*

Dan: You mean the girl part?

Therapist: Exactly. What's happening inside you as I'm sharing all this?

Dan: I'm relaxing. I'm curious. When I'm calm, I can recognize that my reactions are often way bigger than the scenario would justify. But when I'm in it, I feel so justified! [*looks at Cate*] What do you think of this?

Cate: I am thinking about you, but I am also thinking about me and how quickly I react. It's a relief to know we have reasons for doing what we do—and that we might have a way out.

Therapist: You can also help each other in these moments. When we get triggered in a relationship, we often have the experience of feeling alone and unsafe. A couple of important strategies for changing this are learning to unblend and learning a safe and courageous way to communicate your feelings. Would you be interested?

> *Offering the tool of courageous communication (see Section 2)*

Cate: Well this is one of our big goals, isn't it, Dan?

Dan: Yes, it is.

After the therapist helped Cate and Dan address their protectors' fears so these parts could unblend, the session went on.

Therapist: Dan, I wonder if you would like to speak on behalf of any of the parts we've spent time with today?

Dan: I think Cate knows them.

Therapist: She might know them directly, but does she know them through you?

Cate: [*nods*] We're on the receiving end of each other's paranoid, mean parts.

> *Validating and taking responsibility, which creates reciprocity and facilitates ANS regulation (Dana, 2018)*

Dan: Okay. I'll give it a go. For today, Cate, this is what I know. I can be angry and mean. That's a part. He gets triggered when you are critical.

Therapist: Can I restate that? [*Dan nods*] Okay. He gets triggered when you feel criticized.

Dan: Well, okay. Sometimes I experience you that way, Cate.

Cate: I can own that. I can be critical.

Dan: Okay. So it's like this volcano erupts in my body. It's this part who gets enraged and indignant. What I'm hearing is that he is protecting another part who got beat up when I was young. That message was "You are unacceptable." This message is "Never again!" Let's talk about expressing emotion, for example. My family could never understand what was happening with me. No teachers, no friends. No one understood. The bullying was relentless. I was tortured a few times. Did you know I was raped when I was 14? [*Dan begins to cry*]

Therapist: Is it okay to feel this right now?

> *Asking permission to continue*

Dan: [*nods and continues to cry*] It's the part who got hurt. She was so scared and alone! She was brutalized.

Therapist: Can we be with her now?

Dan: I am with her. But I feel these other parts want to bury her.

Therapist: Does that make sense to you?

> *Checking for unblending*

Dan: It does.

Therapist: Is she aware of you?

Dan: She is.

Therapist: What makes sense right now given her needs?

Dan: I want Cate to know about her.

Therapist: Cate, are you available to hear about this part of Dan?

Cate: I am! I've always wondered about this, Dan. It seems like you've had to cut a piece off. [*speaking in a soft tone of voice*] Can I move closer to you?

At this point, Cate moved toward Dan and reached out to touch his knee. Spontaneous touch is a bid for connection and co-regulation.

Dan: I like that. I feel you. She was so trapped, so frantic. Trying to fit in made me… made this part of me sick. My mother could not deal with me… her.

Therapist: How are you experiencing her?

Dan: She looks like a little boy actually. Or should I say, how we identify little boys?

Therapist: How do you feel toward her now?

Dan: Really, really sad.

Therapist: [*to Cate*] What moves you?

Cate: Big sadness. I've heard some stories of course, but not this.

Therapist: We don't have much time left today. I am wondering, Dan, if you could stay inside with this part a little longer?

Dan: [*closes his eyes*] I can tell you this isn't easy given the resistance I feel toward her.

Therapist: Other parts?

Dan: Yes. They are afraid of her.

Therapist: Is there anything you want to say to them?

> *Inviting the client's Self to respond to an inner dilemma*

Dan: Yes. I need to do this. The past haunts us. She needs me. It's time.

Therapist: And how do they respond?

Dan: They're okay right at this moment. But I know this is just the beginning. Right now, there's not a lot of confidence about me doing this.

Therapist: Given that this is the beginning and the process is new, does their doubt make sense to you?

Dan: I get it. I'll need to show up.

Therapist: Let's go back and help the girl find a place that will feel safe and comfortable until we return.

Dan: She wants to stay here, with us.

Therapist: How is that for you?

Dan: Good.

Therapist: Cate, is there anything you want to say to Dan or to this part? From your heart.

> *Asking the partner to provide validation, which helps diminish arousal (Fruzzetti & Worrall, 2010).*

Cate: [*after a pause*] I appreciate you being willing to go there. You do make sense. I wish these things hadn't happened to you. And I want you to know that I know our problems aren't all you, even though I sometimes say you are the problem. The way I see it now, our relationship can only get better if we unwind our miserable childhoods.

❧

This session was complex for a few reasons. Initially, both partners were autonomically aroused. While Cate was able to self-regulate, Dan needed help. Therefore, the therapist focused on supporting him while being careful not to abandon Cate or lose sight of holding them as a couple. Over the course of the session, the therapist educated them about their autonomic nervous systems, helped Dan reach an optimal state of arousal (using the top-down interventions of validation, mirroring, and inviting him to speak for feelings), and then helped him make a U-turn so he could attend internally.

Inside, Dan learned that an angry teenage boy was protecting a terrified girl who looked like a boy and had been exiled internally as well as externally. His system continued to view her as a threat. By regulating his ANS, Dan was able to exhibit a Self-led challenge to this shunning, and he included Cate in his process. He saw that the girl needed rescue and wisely understood that the fears of his other parts would get in the way. This session illustrates how external validation reassures and internal reconnection soothes, helping individuals and couples move from an initial state of dysregulated disconnection toward optimal calm and presence.

When couples like Dan and Cate come to therapy feeling dysregulated—with their protective systems in chronic overdrive—our job is to help them recapture trust. When they feel despair, our job is to be patient and persistent. The steps of IFIO are all designed to support couples in developing safety and trust. The goal is to help them be aware of but not blended with their parts. The more unblended their parts, the more regulated their nervous system. The more regulated the nervous systems of both partners, the more likely they will support instead of abandon each other in times of conflict and distress. A well-regulated nervous system invites relational synchrony, inside and out.

4 Challenges for Therapists

THERAPISTS HAVE PARTS: WHAT'S HARD IN THERAPY IS WHAT'S HARD FOR YOU

Just like clients, we therapists have parts and burdens that can interfere with therapy. Countertransference is an inevitable feature of all relationships. If we are oblivious about our parts and ignore their needs, we make it a problem. But we can make it an opportunity. Judgmental or fearful parts who pop up mark a spot where calm, curious inquiry will produce important knowledge about our parts' needs. Couples are never objectively "easy" or "difficult." For example, our dread of the next session with a withdrawn, uncommunicative couple is a prompt to find and unburden our own exiles. The following issues often cause countertransference reactions. They spring from the therapist's burdens and warrant exploration:

1. **The couple's style of interacting reminds the therapist of their past.**
   - "My parents or caretakers acted this way."

     Parts who had learning experiences with parents or other caretakers during childhood are likely to rouse when a couple exhibits similar behavior. Usually, we're talking about negative experiences from the past, but countertransference knows no bounds. If you particularly loved a grandparent and one member of the couple strikes you as similarly fun or benevolent, countertransference can be no less of an issue. Here, as always, our job is to be mindful of our parts' reactions to our clients' parts, due either to identification or dislike, and to use this information to clear the path and help our exiles unburden so we can be Self-led in our role as therapist.

2. **The couple is navigating an affair or betrayal.**
   - "I was taught to disapprove of infidelity on moral grounds."
   - "I've been hurt or someone I care about has been hurt by an infidelity."

     An individual's response to infidelity (or betrayal) of any kind will depend on what it means to them, which depends on their history and culture. Affairs often mobilize protectors because they involve lies and signal at least some level of abandonment. The meaning a person brings to their partner's infidelity is key. An affair might be taken to mean something shaming, like *I am not enough*, or it might evoke a judgment, like *You are immoral* or *You are bad*. Alternatively, it might highlight a real power differential and mean *I am helpless and cannot protect myself*. In any case, some therapists have strong feelings about infidelity because of their experience in childhood or in romantic relationships later, others will have learned to disapprove, and yet others will have developed strong feelings after witnessing someone else suffering. Our point is the same here as with all hot-button issues. When strong feelings arise, be mindful of your reactivity and help your own parts.

3. The couple presents with sexual problems.

- "I'm not trained for this."
- "Some of my parts are embarrassed by this topic."

   We recommend raising the topic of sex even if your clients don't. Many couples struggle with their sexual relationship, but their parts are too embarrassed to mention it. Although you don't need to be a sex therapist to help a couple explore sex, you do need to feel comfortable talking about sex, exploring it, and listening well to clients. Therefore, knowing when to refer out is also important. If any countertransference issue feels overwhelming because of your experiences, you can get supervision or refer the couple for adjunctive treatment with a specialist. Also, where the body is concerned, you may need to involve medical treatment providers. That said, this is another topic that can mark important concerns in your system, which you will benefit by exploring.

4. Critical, shaming protectors in one or both partners attack the therapist.

- "Yikes! Do I deserve this?"
- "How can I get rid of this client?"
- "They're hopeless."
- "Their problems are endless."
- "They're not motivated to get better."
- "I can't be responsible for someone who acts this way."

   How can we get shamed? Let us count the ways. How do our protectors react? The list here illustrates some commonplace options. Whatever your vulnerabilities may be, a firefighter who is up to snuff will find them. If we are prepared, being shamed by a client's firefighter is an opportunity because they show us what's going on inside us between a critic and exile, and what is being externalized in the direction of the couple. Preparation for shaming involves the usual advice (i.e., find your exiles and help them unburden). But even if all your exiles are perfectly unburdened, shaming is a hurtful behavior, and you can still have parts who take it personally. Therefore, prepare your protectors by reminding them that you are doing a job and that you don't need protecting. If you made a mistake or the client has a valid complaint, admit it and model a repair. A client's part who projects or picks a fight to distract from fear or emotional pain also offers a therapeutic opportunity.

5. Shamed exiles blend in one of the partners and then in the therapist.

- "This is too much for anyone to bear."
- "They [the other partner] are too much."

   Emotional overwhelm is easily transmitted, highlighting the infantile beginning of empathy called emotional contagion. When one baby cries, other babies within earshot cry too. If the therapist has a young exile who feels shameful, identifies with the client's exile, and overwhelms the therapist, then the therapist's protectors will blame the client, believing the client is causing the therapist's pain.

6. A part of the therapist identifies with one partner, takes over internally (blends), and triangulates with the couple.

Couple therapy is inherently triangulating. Once we get triangulated with a couple, we may hear ourselves saying things like:

- "This partner is the problem. That one is balanced."
- "This partner is too controlling; all they do is react."
- "I like this one, but not that one."

Additionally, we may find ourselves doing the following:

- Leaning toward one partner and away from the other.
- Feeling sorry for one partner.
- Identifying with one partner and then becoming protective.
- Taking sides.

> In IFIO, we teach clinicians that couple therapists will unconsciously default to the triangles they negotiated as a child in their family of origin. Our job is to explore and resolve our family-of-origin triangles.

7. The therapist is working with a high-conflict couple.

In the language of IFIO, "high conflict" describes a couple presenting with protectors who feel extremely threatened and who will adopt any strategy to try to create intrapsychic safety. They are committed to their own stories, which usually involve blaming the other person and being right. These protectors have a negative effect on the nervous systems of both partners and the therapist. Because these parts focus exclusively on their idea of safety, they lose perspective quickly and frequently. If the therapist's exiles respond with high anxiety, fear, cognitive overwhelm, or dissociation, the therapist's protectors will say things like:

- "I can't handle them."
- "They should divorce."
- "They are pathological."
- "How can I fire them?"
- "I can't help them."

> As always, our job is to know and help our exiles. If we need time to do that, or we are, for some other reason, not in a position to help a couple, we have a responsibility to address the fears and judgments of our parts and refer the couple with kindness.

8. Protectors react negatively to parts language or refuse to allow a U-turn.

- "I am helpless with this couple because they haven't signed on for help and they don't cooperate."

> A client's protective parts can refuse to budge for many reasons. Often, they feel misunderstood, disrespected, or invalidated. Some fear that parts language will threaten their control of the internal system, and some have had a negative experience in past therapy. Because these protectors can seem implacable, therapist parts who need to feel successful can become intolerant of them.

9. Dysregulated parts of the therapist emerge.

The IFIO motto is "we are them." Therapists have parts and a Self. We have childhood wounds, relational histories, divorces, and so on. When the therapist's burdens from unhealed relationship traumas activate with a couple in session, the therapist can transform from a well-regulated, unblended guide to a frightened, overwhelmed child. No worries. With awareness, commitment, and practice, we can help our parts unblend consistently. Consultation is a good idea for some cases. If any of the following feelings or thoughts start repeating, it's time for your own U-turn:

- "These people overwhelm me."
- "I am too anxious to be effective."
- "It's their fault."
- "They remind me of my parents."
- "Their trauma mirrors mine."
- "I hate couple therapy."
- "I'm incompetent."

POTENTIALLY HOT TOPICS IN COUPLE THERAPY

Certain topics are more likely to bring up strong feelings in the therapist. These include:

- Sex and sexuality. For example:
  - A polyamorous couple seeks help from a therapist who believes in monogamy.
  - A couple in which one partner has had affairs and lied seeks help from a therapist who has not recovered from the infidelity of a partner or parent.
- Gender. For example:
  - A couple with one or two trans partners seeks help from a cisgendered therapist whose beliefs are implicitly or explicitly biased regarding gender assignment at birth.
- Diversity and inclusion. For example:
  - Couples of color seek help from a white therapist who is implicitly or explicitly racially biased.
  - A biracial couple seeks help from a therapist of the same race as one partner and different from the other (or different from both partners), who is implicitly or explicitly racially biased.
- Religious, cultural, or political differences. For example:
  - A Catholic couple who is anti-abortion seeks help from a non-Catholic therapist who is pro-choice, and one or all of them are implicitly or explicitly biased toward people who hold different opinions.
  - A couple who disagrees about abortion seeks help from a therapist who agrees with one partner but not the other.
  - A Hasidic couple seeks help from a non-Hasidic therapist who believes that women need to be educated and equally empowered in relationships, or vice versa.
  - A couple who voted for Donald Trump seeks help from a therapist who supported Elizabeth Warren, or vice versa.

Regardless of the couple's presenting issue, and even when therapists feel reactive in response to a client, the IFIO protocol remains the same. This is also true of IFS, which is why therapists have used the IFS approach successfully with all kinds of populations across a wide variety of settings. When it comes to our personal experiences, we all inhabit specific, narrow perspectives. We also unconsciously generalize from our personal experiences, sometimes more accurately than other times. This is why the therapist's job in both IFIO and IFS is to maintain a continual U-turn stance, a kind of flowing assessment of our own level of blending and access to the Self's broad views. One of the hallmarks of the Self is having the ability to encompass multiple perspectives at once. When we do a U-turn and unblend (with the help of supervision, if necessary), we notice our responses to clients and we are more available to them.

That said, it behooves the therapist to be—or become—knowledgeable about the specifics of a couple's presenting problems. Clients always teach us about themselves, but it is not their responsibility to spend their time teaching us about issues we can learn on our own through reading and consultation. Some clients have specific requirements of a therapist (e.g., the therapist must be gay or African American), some prioritize their feelings about the therapist over any other consideration, and others steer clear of experts purposely because they want to guide their therapist's thinking on topics of importance to them. If a couple somehow ends up in your office and wants something you can't give, you can offer to get supervision and read up, or you can refer them.

Sometimes we want to involve other treatment providers. For example, it's wise for clients to get a professional assessment for medical issues, though it's also a good idea to explore if (and to what extent) parts might be involved with the problem. Expert advice can also be important to functional issues, like certain sexual problems. A life-threatening problem, like some addictions and eating disorders, may also require medical expertise. But even if you refer one or both partners to another provider for their expertise, the couple may want to continue seeing you.

The following worksheet can help therapists explore and get in touch with any parts who contribute to personal patterns of reactivity in sessions with clients. IFIO therapists must keep countertransference in mind and notice if they are having strong reactions to one or both partners. Without this degree of mindfulness, a therapist's reactive protectors or frightened exiles will confuse the therapeutic relationship and block progress. In fact, when therapy stalls, explore countertransference first. It's likely to be the problem.

Therapist Worksheet

THERAPIST PARTS:
RESPONDING TO OUR OWN REACTIVITY

All therapists get caught in their own dilemmas during therapy. As a rule, from the beginning of treatment, we ask therapists to be curious about their own responses to the partners in a couple. The following questions will help you be curious when your parts get reactive.

1. What sensations do you feel in your body? Describe their location, their intensity, and the movement of their energy.

   _____

   _____

2. What are your initial impulses (e.g., flight, fight, run, hide, numb, laugh, collapse, give up, protect)?

   _____

   _____

3. What do your parts say to you?

   _____

   _____

4. Identify and describe your protectors, either managers or firefighters.

   _____

   _____

5. Identify and describe your exiles.

   _____

   _____

6. Look back over your notes to identify any parts who react predictably and repeatedly. Would they be willing to meet your Self? What would help them be willing to unblend?

   _____

   _____

Copyright © 2021, Toni Herbine-Blank, Martha Sweezy, *Internal Family Systems Couple Therapy Skills Manual*. All rights reserved.

5 Experiential Exercises:
Reenactments, Rescripting, and Repair

Protectors who are in the habit of fighting, fleeing, or freezing in pursuit of safety interfere with a couple's ability to attune and be the mutually loving resource each of them needs. Experiential exercises, which involve less talk and more focus on the body, are a great way for couples to deepen their internal and external understanding by doing something different. We help them move beyond considering change to having new, powerfully integrating experiences.

The experiential exercises here involve reenacting and rescripting a painful interchange. As with any model of therapy, practice highlights further possibilities. Therefore, once you have absorbed the basic tools of the IFIO approach, we encourage you to trust your intuition and develop more experiential exercises.

EXPERIENTIAL PLAY

Creative rescripting helps couples deactivate their ANS, repair misunderstandings and miscommunications, and change entrenched relational patterns. It also buoys hope and reveals more material to explore. The willingness of partners to try a new behavior depends, in our view, on their protectors being willing to unblend and concede that a new behavior might help. Inner differentiation gives each partner more space to do the essential U-turn and notice their own parts' dilemmas. Once the Self is differentiated from their parts, we want each of them to be more involved with their own internal systems. Ironically, this inner attentiveness helps them accept and be kind toward their partner's struggles. Kindness inside launches a beneficial cycle and prepares partners to be kind to each other by interrupting hurtful patterns on their own between sessions.

With experiential exercises, we ask partners to move out of their comfort zones and try something different. These exercises slow everything down and help partners embody a dilemma that they can work out in vivo with the therapist's help. We introduce experiments when we judge that the couple's mutual trust level is high enough and we feel confident that an experiment will be instructive.

Borrowing from Gestalt therapy, the following therapist handout contains two experiments that guide clients to learn by doing (Roubal, 2009). These experiments are creative and adventurous. They can be simple or complex depending on the situation and the couple's level of comfort. They aim to help each partner unblend, see how they behave in conflict, and—by embodying their partner's parts—understand and empathize with their partner. Once the experiment is launched, we go with the flow. Our guiding instruction is to hold agendas for specific outcomes lightly so we can be open, curious, and Self-led. The experience helps us understand strong feelings in the present, and it may reveal important issues for future attention.[*]

---

[*] We thank Noëlle Buffière for her assistance in developing these experiments.

Therapist Worksheet

EXPERIMENTING WITH EXPERIENCES:
Re-Enactment

To set up the following two experiments, begin by asking the couple if they are interested in experimenting, and describe what you have in mind. Create safety during this process by noticing first if you have the confidence to stay present for whatever happens. If not, help your parts unblend. Then get permission from the couple to try something new and welcome resistant parts.

During an experiment, pay attention to moments when a partner's inquiry could deepen, and encourage them to express vulnerability. Help them anchor their experiences by continually asking what they notice and what's happening in their bodies.

Finally, leave time for processing individual and relational experiences.

Experiment #1: Doing a U-Turn

1. Invite the couple to choose and describe an incident to focus on. Choose an incident that evoked strong sensations, feelings, and thoughts in one or both partners. Before proceeding, help them decide what they can agree on about the event, and remind them that memory is inaccurate, especially when coupled with strong feelings.

2. Invite the partners to stand and move around the room if they're willing.

3. Negotiate whose experience will be attended to first. We will call this person Partner A.

4. Invite both to go inside (do a U-turn) and ask protectors to unblend so each partner can find the parts who were involved with the event in question.

5. Check to see if Partner B is aware of their parts and can stay present to listen.

6. Then direct your attention to Partner A and ask, "What did Partner B say or do at the time that triggered this cascade of sensations, feelings, and thoughts?"

7. Tell Partner A that you are going to ask Partner B to reenact that triggering behavior, and ask Partner A to notice:

   • Their body

   • What they hear their parts saying internally

   • Their feelings

Copyright © 2021, Toni Herbine-Blank, Martha Sweezy, *Internal Family Systems Couple Therapy Skills Manual*. All rights reserved.

- The part who seems most vulnerable in this situation

8. Then ask Partner B to reenact the triggering behavior.

    • Check in with Partner A during this time. Did they notice the vulnerable part under their reactivity? Take a moment to explore its hopes, fears, and needs.

9. Check in with Partner B:

    • What was it like to act that way again?

    • What did they notice about their parts?

    • What feelings come up now?

10. Now (if there's time) or in the next session, reverse roles and repeat the sequence.

Experiment #2: Going Deeper: Becoming the Other

With the aim of helping partners truly understand each other and gain a broader perspective on their dynamic, this experiment goes beyond role reversal by asking each partner to use their imagination to embody the other partner and feel into the other's parts. This experiment begins with the initial steps of experiment #1:

1. Ask Partner A, "What did your partner say or do at the time that triggered this cascade of sensations, feelings, and thoughts?"

2. Invite Partner B to reenact the trigger behavior while Partner A notices:

    o Their body

    o What they hear their parts saying internally

    o Their feelings

    o The part who seems most vulnerable in this situation

3. Check in with Partner B:

    o What was it like to act that way again?

    o What did they notice about their parts?

    o How do they feel now?

4. Now, instead of simply reversing roles, ask Partner A to imagine *being* Partner B. Slow this way down. Explain that Partner A will repeat the triggering behavior while noticing their body, what they hear inside, and what they feel. Then invite Partner A to enact the triggering behavior.

5. Now explore what Partner A noticed while doing the behavior, and ask Partner A to speak for the wishes and needs of Partner B's parts.

Copyright © 2021, Toni Herbine-Blank, Martha Sweezy, *Internal Family Systems Couple Therapy Skills Manual.* All rights reserved.

6. Next, ask what Partner B noticed about being in Partner A's shoes, and ask Partner B to speak for the wishes and needs of Partner A's parts.

7. Ask each partner to speak for the experience of being in the other's shoes:

   • What have they learned?

   • What surprised them?

   • Did they notice any projections? That is, anything that belonged to them rather than the other person?

   • Take time to explore how this might inform future inquiry.

8. Finally, invite them to rescript their original interaction to see how it goes now.

9. Take time to note new insights before stopping.

Copyright © 2021, Toni Herbine-Blank, Martha Sweezy, *Internal Family Systems Couple Therapy Skills Manual*. All rights reserved.

BECOMING THE OTHER

The following vignette illustrates a rescripting sequence in which a couple first reversed roles and then became each other. The couple, Kim and Dave, had been married for 17 years. They were cisgendered, heterosexual, in their fifties, and had two school-age children. Kim, who was biracial (a European-American mother and an African-American father), was raised in England. Dave, who was African American, was raised in the United States. Kim's job as a lawyer required her to travel at least five days a month. Dave, who was a tenured professor at a local university, did not travel regularly.

Kim seemed comfortable in therapy sessions, given that she had been in therapy in the past and her mother was a psychologist. Dave, on the other hand, had never been in therapy and was initially concerned about his reputation at the university and the stigma of having mental health issues. They expressed a great deal of goodwill toward each other, parented together well, reported good communication, and generally felt satisfied in their relationship. But they had not been able to break a pattern of quarreling whenever Kim returned home from a business trip. These fights were quick and painful.

The first few therapy sessions, which were rich and proved helpful for everyone, focused on their feelings about working with the therapist, a cisgendered, lesbian, European American, who grew up in the United States. The next focus was on hearing from Dave's parts, who were wary of therapy. This went well. Both partners found that parts language helped their protectors unblend so they could notice vulnerable exiles, and they appreciated learning how their nervous systems were functioning during stressful conversations. Dave learned that he had parts who tended to fight and then flee, while Kim had parts who tended to shut down quickly. They were quick to use the tools the therapist taught them to help these protectors unblend. The following session illustrates an experiment in which they reenacted and then rescripted a typical fight.

Kim: We're still struggling with this thing we get into when I get back from a trip. It's sad. I feel so ready to come home. I've missed Dave and the kids. And then this difficult dynamic happens. I'm exhausted by the travel, and I don't cope with it well.

Therapist: And this is where you want to focus today?

Kim: It is.

Therapist: [*to Dave*] Okay with you?

Dave: Yes. It's fresh in our minds. Kim just got back from being on the West Coast for longer than usual.

Therapist: [*to Dave*] Any more you want to speak for about that?

Dave: I feel pretty upset. I notice that I felt criticized and dismissed. And then I got dismissive.

Therapist: Who would like to start unpacking this dilemma?

Kim: [*to Dave*] Since you're upset right now, do you want to start?

Dave: Sure.

Therapist: [*to Dave*] Let me just remind you that you'll be speaking for your experience and that memory is distorted by strong feelings. [*turning to Kim*] And you'll have the chance to fill in when Dave finishes.

Kim: Fair enough.

Dave: Okay. So, as we've discussed, my sensibility about housekeeping is different from Kim's. As far as she's concerned, when she's away and I'm in charge, things go to hell in a handbasket. I'm disorganized, and the kids are all over the place, so the house ends up being chaotic. I do my absolute best to get everything together before she gets home because I know she will get tweaked when things aren't perfect. But the minute she walks in, she notices the chaos rather than what I've done to pull it together. She seems frustrated; I feel dismissed. I get pissed off and remove myself. I take it really personally.

Therapist: [*to Kim*] Want to add?

Kim: Well, I hear that, and I know all that. But his story is that I want things to be perfect. And while it's true that I spot it when things are out of place, and I do get tweaked or start micromanaging him and the kids, his response is unkind. He can be mean. I'm exhausted from travel and putting out about a 150 percent of my energy for days on end. I come home looking forward to some rest and peace. So I don't like this part of me, the one who sees the chaos and forgets the effort (thank you Mother!), but I also don't like Dave's response. I get pissed and kind of lecture-y with him. He sulks off, and I storm off. Then I shut down and hear myself saying things like "Why do I even bother coming home?" I guess I just feel lonely.

Therapist: This pattern is recognizable, yes? [*both nod*] I have an idea. If you're game, let's unpack this scenario in a different way right now. Let's do it over in slow motion so you can discover what's under your reactions to each other and feel into each other's experiences. This exercise is like tracking your fights and understanding what your protectors do or say, but it's more in depth.

> (Introducing the couple to the idea)

Kim: Can you say more?

Therapist: I'll be asking you to stand and move around. [*Dave winces*] Of course, you don't have to do it that way. I'll give you choices.

Dave: No, I'll try. If it's too strange, I'll let you know.

Therapist: Great. I'll invite you to go back to what happened earlier this week and reenact it from when Kim comes in the door. I'll ask you both to notice all the parts who are engaged in the situation, and we will pause as needed to ask them to unblend.

> (Creating safety by going into more detail about the exercise)

Kim: I'm up for it. Dave?

Dave: Sure.

Therapist: Although I have an idea about how this will go, we're exploring, and, as you've probably noticed, anything can happen. So we'll see where it takes us. Okay? [*they nod*] Stand up and place yourselves anywhere in the room. Dave, can we start with you?

Dave: Sure.

Therapist: [*to Kim*] For now, I'm going to coach you. Let's start with noticing any parts who may not want to hear from Dave and asking them to unblend. Then take a scan of your body, and make sure you have enough space to listen.

(*Offering help*)

Kim: [*closes her eyes, takes a moment inside, then opens her eyes*] Believe it or not, I am pretty available. I think we both play a part in this, and I feel embarrassed about being so critical.

Therapist: You have a part who can be critical?

(*Reframing with parts language*)

Kim: I do.

Therapist: I am going to ask you to come in the room and do or say what you normally do or says that gets to Dave.

Kim: [*stands at the opposite end of the room and walks toward Dave*] Hi honey!

Dave: Welcome home!

Dave gives her a hug. Kim simulates taking off her coat and searching for a hanger. Then she turns to Dave and speaks in an irritated tone.

Kim: Why are there these shoes dumped all over the closet? And why are there no hangers for my coat?

Therapist: Dave, take a moment to notice what's happening in your body.

Dave: Yup, there it is! The part who gets pissed.

Therapist: What do you hear it saying? Take your time.

Dave: It doesn't matter how hard I try. I can't get it right! I have been working tirelessly to get this house cleaned up for Kim. It's never going to happen.

Therapist: This part is afraid it's never going to get this right.

(*Reframing with parts language*)

Dave: Yes.

Therapist: And what does that mean about you?

Dave: I'm inadequate.

Therapist: And when you feel inadequate what happens?

Dave: I get mad.

Therapist: And then you notice an impulse to move away from Kim?

Dave: That's right.

Therapist: Can you feel those urges to fight and flee in your body?

Naming the autonomic response

Dave: I feel those energies running right through me.

Therapist: [*to Kim*] How are you doing?

Kim: Good. I just want to listen right now.

Dave: You're not tweaked by this?

Kim: Not at the moment.

Therapist: [*to Kim*] Are you available to hear more?

Kim: I sure am. Though I want to make sure Dave will listen to me at some point.

Therapist: Of course. We'll reverse roles later today or, if we don't have time today, in another session. [*to Dave*] You have a lot of energy in your body. Would it help to move?

Reassuring protectors

Dave: As a matter of fact, yes! [*he paces and shakes his arms, then stops and takes a deep breath*] Okay I feel better. I still notice a strong desire to get away. It's weird to pay this much attention to my body.

Therapist: [*to Kim*] What's happening with you?

Kim: I can relate to having all that energy in my body and then getting stuck trying to figure it out mentally.

Therapist: Dave, can we keep going with your parts? [*Dave nods*] As you pay attention to the sensations in your body, can you find what's underneath all the energy?

Dave: [*to Kim*] I feel hurt. That's the bottom line. I just don't get why some correction or annoyance has to be the very first thing out of your mouth when you get home.

Therapist: It makes sense that you want to ask Kim this question, Dave, but first can you speak more for that hurt? We'll get to your questions.

Dave: I feel the hurt. [*to Kim*] I am trying to take care of you by doing what doesn't come naturally to me—but it's never enough, and that hurts. This is a vulnerable thing to admit. I've worked so hard in so many areas of my life to get it right, but the place where it's most important, I always fail. I don't think you get how hard I try. You don't see what I do.

Therapist: [*to Kim*] What's happening?

Kim: I feel guilty. I do have a part who feels out of control about this, but it's not that you aren't enough.

Therapist: [*to Kim*] Given what Dave has revealed about his childhood, does the burden he's describing of never getting it right make sense to you?

Kim: Yes certainly.

Therapist: [*to Dave*] What's it like to hear that?

Dave: Good, actually.

Therapist: Dave, do you have a request for Kim?

Dave: I do. I want you to greet us before you start talking about what annoys you and before you start moving things around to take care of yourself. I want you to see what's right before you look for what isn't. Does that make sense?

Kim: It really does, Dave. We joke around that I have an OCD part, but I think we're onto something. Maybe not OCD per se, but something like that. It's my struggle. I am committed to working on it. I don't want to hurt you or put the kids in the crossfire.

Therapist: Right now, Dave, what's it like for your parts to be seen and heard?

Dave: Way better. Thank you. [*turns to Kim*] Thank you, Kim, for hearing me and agreeing to work on this.

Therapist: We have some time left. [*to Dave*] Are you available to learn about Kim's experience?

Dave: Very.

Therapist: This time I'm going to ask you to do something a little different. I want you to reverse roles. To get a sense of what goes on inside Kim, you will stand in her shoes. Okay?

> *Telling them the plan and asking for permission*

Dave: Sounds okay to me.

Kim: I love this idea!

Therapist: Stand up again, Dave. Feel your feet on the floor, close your eyes, and find your inner Kim. Start with what she was feeling when she arrived home.

Dave: Tired, happy to be home, looking forward to seeing us. [*Kim nods*] So I come inside, get a hug from Dave, open the closet to hand my coat up, and my heart sinks. In my head I hear, "What about me?" The shoes are a jumble on the closet floor, and I can't even find a hanger. I'm tired, and now I'm thinking about having to clean up after everyone the minute I get home. I feel disappointed and lonely.

Therapist: Great, Dave. You can open your eyes now. What was that like for you?

Dave: Sad. She comes home tired, but she wants to be home again—and then it's ruined for her.

Therapist: Okay to go a little deeper? Close your eyes again and find her parts.

> *Deepening the inquiry*

Dave: [*closes his eyes and is quiet for a few seconds*] I sense a need to be taken care of. And maybe some feelings of being overwhelmed and out of control. [*opens his eyes and looks at Kim*] Am I getting this right?

Kim: Exactly right. Then my irritated part steps in to hide that.

Dave: And then my irritated part reacts.

Therapist: Kim, what's it like to hear Dave now?

Kim: Great. Isn't it amazing that we feel just about the same way?

Therapist: And since these internal conversations drive your external conversations, how would it be to speak for that with each other? And even make a regular exercise of putting yourselves in each other's shoes?

Dave: I really like this exercise. I got to something important today. I'd be willing to try it at home.

Therapist: Having stood in Kim's shoes, what do you think she needs most?

Dave: To be understood.

Kim: And for you to be kind when you call me on something.

Dave: Makes sense. I guess that would involve me not feeling victimized.

Therapist: That's right. My invitation is for you to cultivate your open heart even when your partner is blended with a reactive part. I understand that speaking for underlying needs can be challenging when one or both of you feels reactive. But as you gain more understanding about your inner dilemmas, you'll recognize your partner's dilemmas too, and compassion will take over from all that reactivity. Let me say just one last thing today. I hear the vulnerability under your protectors. A part of you, Kim, says, "What about me?" And a part of you, Dave, says, "Do you see me?" These are important parts. We'll come back to them next time.

> *Providing an overview and inviting them to explore new material in the future*

As this example illustrates, experiments that move beyond the basic steps of IFIO enliven sessions with couples. This experiential exercise involved replaying a troubled interaction, slowing both partners down to do a U-turn and observe their parts, doing the scene over, and, finally, doing it again in reversed roles. It allowed them to explore their inner world, talk about what they discovered safely, and try new behaviors. Reenactments and role reversals develop a couple's awareness of alternatives while building their understanding and self-acceptance (Yaniv, 2018). The experience can lead to spontaneous repair. Additionally, the information we glean from the exercise gives direction for future sessions.

Conclusion

As this book illustrates, IFIO has specific aims but is not time limited. It is organized into a beginning, a middle, and an end. In the beginning, we ask a few key questions. What do these partners hope for, what do they fear, and what are their goals for therapy? Since we aim to help them feel safe differentiating so they can attach, we assess how they view sameness and difference. We also ask them if they would like help to be fully themselves while staying securely connected in their relationship.

In the middle of IFIO therapy, the length of which we cannot predict, we help the couple differentiate in two relational realms, one outside and the other inside. First, we assess their patterns of behavior and interactions while guiding them to notice their parts. Then we help them differentiate from their parts and from each other with unblending skills, especially speaking *for* rather than *from* their parts, and listening from the heart without judging, panicking about erasure, or trying to exert control.

UNBLENDING IS THE KEY TO THIS THERAPY

Unblending changes the speaker's tone and the listener's way of hearing. It makes room for the partners to be curious about protective parts. As they discover that they both have exiles under all that protection, they are able to empathize, validate, and extend compassion, bearing witness to early wounding and laying the groundwork for relational unburdening. This process brings them to the last hurdle of treatment: apology, repair, and (if it's in the cards) forgiveness, from a place of gratitude and mutual respect.

All couples need skills for renewing secure connection. The components of a good apology include evidence that the transgressor can unblend from protectors, take care of their exiles, and take responsibility for any damage that's been done. The ability to have a skillful discussion about forgiveness requires everything we teach, especially good access to the Self, and comes last for most couples. We have suggested reviewing three points with the couple before diving into that discussion. First, forgiving does not dictate the future; couples may forgive but decide to part ways. Second, forgiving does not undo or erase the past. Rather, it signals that the injured partner has accepted their own vulnerability and made a unilateral decision to help their protectors step down. Third, forgiving activates grief. If a protector confuses grief with depression, it will need to be reassured about the importance and safety of mourning.

When our parts feel loved, our hearts open to others. However, they cannot feel our love unless they unblend. Likewise, partners must differentiate to give and receive love. We help the couple differentiate and reconnect by helping each partner do a U-turn and unblend from parts. IFIO is a differentiation model of psychotherapy. We are not asking partners to be islands and meet all their own needs or to be stoic and alone, as some parts may fear. Rather, we know that the couple's desire to be together and their ability to meet each other's emotional needs will strengthen as their parts feel better connected with their Self.

Our job is to help clients do something new. We want couples to experience being separate and connected, different and acceptable, supportive and self-reliant, unique and together. We give them the opportunity to speak for their anger, desire, grief, and love. We invite them to apologize and ask forgiveness. We help them be their own best problem solvers. In IFIO therapy, couples discover that there is no contradiction between caring for their parts and caring for their mate; there is always room for me *and* you. IFIO does not specify one route to loving, nor does it dictate a time frame. Whatever the couple finds mutually satisfying is what we want for them. But it does offer therapists some effective tools for guiding couples to their goals, including tracking relational dynamics, unblending, and using many routes to the U-turn. We all have core needs, including the needs to individuate, feel safe, express ourselves fully, be in connection, and feel loved. Rebuilding broken bridges and finding their way back to connection helps intimate partners heal old wounds and welcome love with open hearts.

References

For your convenience, purchasers of the book can download the worksheets and handouts at www.pesi.com/IFIO

Anderson, F. G., Sweezy, M., & Schwartz, R. D. (2017). *Internal family systems skills training manual: Trauma-informed treatment for anxiety, depression, PTSD & substance abuse.* Eau Claire, WI: PESI Publishing & Media.

Badenoch, B. (2008). *Being a brain-wise therapist: A practical guide to interpersonal neurobiology.* New York: Norton.

Barstow, C. (2005). *Right use of power: The heart of ethics.* Boulder, CO: Many Realms Publishing.

Cozolino, L. J. (2006). *The neuroscience of human relationships: Attachment and the developing social brain.* New York: W. W. Norton.

Cozolino, L. J. (2008, September/October). It's a jungle in there. *Psychotherapy Networker, 32*(4), 20–27.

Dana, D. (2018). *The polyvagal theory in therapy: Engaging the rhythm of regulation.* New York: W. W. Norton.

Fruzzetti, A. E., & Worrall, J. M. (2010). Accurate expression and validating responses: A transactional model for understanding individual and relationship distress. In K. T. Sullivan & J. Davila (Eds.), *Support processes in intimate relationships* (pp. 121–150). New York: Oxford University Press.

Geib, P. (2016). Expanded unburdenings: Relaxing managers and releasing creativity. In M. Sweezy & E. L. Ziskind (Eds.), *Innovations and elaborations in internal family systems therapy* (pp. 148–163). New York: Routledge.

Hendrix, H. (1988). *Getting the love you want.* New York: Henry Holt and Company.

Herbine-Blank, T., Kerpelman, D. M., & Sweezy, M. (2016). *Intimacy from the inside out: Courage and compassion in couple therapy.* New York: Routledge.

Katie, B. (n.d.). *The work of Byron Katie.* Retrieved from https://thework.com.

Krause, P. K. (2013). IFS with children and adolescents. In M. Sweezy & E. L. Ziskind (Eds.), *Internal family systems therapy: New dimensions* (pp. 35–54). New York: Routledge.

Lewis, H. B. (1974). *Shame and guilt in neurosis.* New York: International Universities Press.

Minuchin, S., & Fishman, H. C. (1981). *Family therapy techniques.* Cambridge, MA: Harvard University Press.

Porges, S. W. (2007). The polyvagal perspective. *Biological Psychology, 74*(2), 116–143.

Roubal, J. (2009). Experiment: A creative phenomenon of the field. *Gestalt Review, 13*(3), 263–276.

Schore, J. R., & Schore, A. N. (2007). Modern attachment theory: The central role of affect regulation in development and treatment. *Clinical Social Work Journal, 36*(1), 9–20.

Schwartz, R. C., & Sweezy, M. (2019). *Internal family systems therapy* (2nd ed.). New York: Guilford Press.

Siegel, D. J. (1999). *The developing mind: Toward a neurobiology of interpersonal experience.* New York: Guilford Press.

Siegel, D. J. (2003). An interpersonal neurobiology of psychotherapy: The developing mind and the resolution of trauma. In M. Solomon & D. J. Siegel (Eds.), *Healing trauma: Attachment, mind, body, and brain* (pp. 1–56). New York: W. W. Norton.

Siegel, D. J. (2007). *The mindful brain: Reflection and attunement in the cultivation of well-being.* New York: W. W. Norton.

Spring, J. A. (2004). *How can I forgive you? The courage to forgive, the freedom not to.* New York: HarperCollins.

Yaniv, D. (2018). Trust the process: A new scientific outlook on psychodramatic spontaneity training. *Frontiers in Psychology, 9,* Article 2083.

Made in United States
Orlando, FL
20 November 2024

54183731R00074